Cambridge Elements

Elements in Current Archaeological Tools and Techniques
edited by
Hans Barnard
Cotsen Institute of Archaeology
Willeke Wendrich
Polytechnic University of Turin

INFRARED SPECTROSCOPY OF ARCHAEOLOGICAL SEDIMENTS

Michael B. Toffolo

Spanish National Research Centre for Human Evolution (CENIEH)

COTSEN INSTITUTE OF
ARCHAEOLOGY AT UCLA

CAMBRIDGE
UNIVERSITY PRESS

Shaftesbury Road, Cambridge CB2 8EA, United Kingdom

One Liberty Plaza, 20th Floor, New York, NY 10006, USA

477 Williamstown Road, Port Melbourne, VIC 3207, Australia

314–321, 3rd Floor, Plot 3, Splendor Forum, Jasola District Centre, New Delhi – 110025, India

103 Penang Road, #05–06/07, Visioncrest Commercial, Singapore 238467

Cambridge University Press is part of Cambridge University Press & Assessment, a department of the University of Cambridge.

We share the University's mission to contribute to society through the pursuit of education, learning and research at the highest international levels of excellence.

www.cambridge.org

Information on this title: www.cambridge.org/9781009532976

DOI: 10.1017/9781009387590

First published 2025

A catalogue record for this publication is available from the British Library

ISBN 978-1-009-53297-6 Hardback
ISBN 978-1-009-38756-9 Paperback
ISSN 2632-7031 (online)
ISSN 2632-7023 (print)

Additional resources for this publication at www.cambridge.org/Toffolo

Infrared Spectroscopy of Archaeological Sediments

Elements in Current Archaeological Tools and Techniques

DOI: 10.1017/9781009387590
First published online: January 2025

Michael B. Toffolo
Spanish National Research Centre for Human Evolution (CENIEH)

Author for correspondence: Michael B. Toffolo, michael.toffolo@cenieh.es,
michael.toffolo@u-bordeaux-montaigne.fr

Abstract: Infrared spectroscopy is the study of the interaction between infrared radiation and matter. Its application to the characterization of archaeological sedimentary contexts has produced invaluable insights into the archaeological record and past human activities. This Element aims at providing a practical guide to infrared spectroscopy of archaeological sediments and their contents taken as a dynamic system, in which the different components observed today are the result of multiple formation processes that took place over long timescales. After laying out the history and fundamentals of the discipline, the author proposes a step-by-step methodological framework, both in the field and the laboratory, and guides the reader in the interpretation of the infrared spectra of the main components of archaeological sediments with the aid of selected case studies. This title is also available as Open Access on Cambridge Core.

Keywords: infrared spectroscopy, microarchaeology, geoarchaeology, archaeological science, sediment

ISBNs: 9781009532976 (HB), 9781009387569 (PB), 9781009387590 (OC)
ISSNs: 2632-7031 (online), 2632-7023 (print)

Contents

1 Introduction

Infrared spectroscopy is a branch of molecular spectroscopy that investigates the interaction of infrared radiation with matter, be it gas, liquid, or solid. When irradiated with infrared light, molecules in a substance vibrate and/or rotate in different ways depending on the nature of the atoms, the strength, length, and symmetry of their bonds with other atoms, and the overall spatial arrangement. Each vibration translates into an absorption at a specific wavelength in the infrared region of the electromagnetic radiation, resulting in a spectrum that exhibits absorption bands characteristic of specific molecules. Therefore, infrared spectroscopy is able to identify organic and inorganic compounds, including in heterogeneous mixtures, as is the case for the sediments that are found at archaeological sites (Weiner 2010).

Infrared light was discovered in 1800, when Sir William Herschel proved that there is a form of light able to carry heat that propagates at frequencies lower than those of the visible spectrum (Herschel 1800). This discovery became relevant to the field of materials science in the 1930s, when the first infrared spectrometers were developed based on the demand for analytical work in the synthetic rubber industry (Derrick *et al.* 1999). These instruments were of the dispersive type, based on a monochromator that requires long acquisition times in order to obtain an infrared spectrum. In the 1950s, a major technological breakthrough in infrared spectroscopy was the introduction of the Michelson interferometer, a device that produces an interferogram in a much shorter span of time, which is then converted into an infrared spectrum by applying a Fourier transform – hence the acronym FTIR, which stands for Fourier transform infrared spectroscopy. By the 1970s, the combination of FTIR spectrometers with a dedicated computer significantly reduced spectrum acquisition times and thus made these instruments more commercially viable, and applications in materials science, biomineralization, medicine, heritage conservation, and archaeometry gained momentum (van der Marel & Beutelspacher 1976; Schrader 1995; Derrick *et al.* 1999).

The systematic application of FTIR spectroscopy to the study of archaeological sediments was pioneered in the 1980s by Steve Weiner, who used this method to study bone preservation and the integrity of the archaeological record at prehistoric cave sites in Israel. Furthermore, he demonstrated that infrared spectrometers can be successfully operated on site, a major advantage in terms of real-time information for the adjustment of excavation and sampling strategies (Weiner & Goldberg 1990). In the following years, FTIR spectroscopy became one of the most important methods in the field of microarchaeology, which is the investigation of the invisible archaeological record (Weiner 2010), and saw the development of major applications in the study of diagenetic processes at archaeological sites, prehistoric and ancient pyrotechnology, and the molecular integrity of materials used in paleoenvironmental reconstructions and absolute dating (Monnier 2018).

While some manuals about FTIR spectroscopy of artworks and archaeological materials have been published in the past three decades (e.g., Derrick *et al.* 1999; Boyatzis 2022), as well as review articles of applications of FTIR in archaeology and other disciplines (e.g., Kirkbride 2009; Gaffney *et al.* 2012; Margaris 2014; Berna 2017; Shoval 2017; Monnier 2018; Toffolo & Berna 2018), to date the only guide to the interpretation of spectra of the main components found in archaeological sediments is that of Weiner (2010: 275–316). This Element aims at providing up-to-date information on the most recent developments in FTIR spectroscopy of archaeological sediments, including the grinding curve method and advances in the study of diagenesis and pyrotechnology. This is done based on the interpretation of the spectra of the most important components of archaeological sediments, which are displayed in both transmission and attenuated total reflectance (ATR) modes.

2 Theoretical and Methodological Framework

This section illustrates the basic concepts of infrared spectroscopy that form the base for the interpretation of spectra, and provides an overview of the instrument setup, sample collection guidelines, and the acquisition of spectra in different modes, including microspectroscopy. Finally, it provides the means of extracting archaeological information from the analysis of spectra.

2.1 Fundamentals of Infrared Spectroscopy

The existence of infrared radiation was demonstrated by Herschel (1800), who discovered it in a clever experiment. While investigating the amount of heat carried by the different components of sunlight, he decided to measure the temperature of colors in the visible light spectrum by passing sunlight through a prism and placing thermometers on a table where the different colors were cast. For each color, he took control measurements of temperatures in the shade. In the process, he also took a measurement beyond the red end of the visible spectrum, and found that the temperature was one degree higher compared to red light. Based on this observation, he concluded that there must be a type of invisible light able to carry heat, which was later named infrared, from the Latin word *infra*, which means "below." Research works that followed found that infrared light is a type of electromagnetic radiation characterized by wavelengths between microwaves and the visible spectrum (e.g., Schrader 1995).

Depending on the wavelength, different types of interactions between electromagnetic radiation and matter may be probed, and their study is called molecular (or atomic) spectroscopy. Since infrared radiation produces vibrational transitions, it is part of the vibrational spectroscopy branch of molecular spectroscopy (together with Raman spectroscopy). The infrared spectrum is further subdivided into the near-infrared (NIR) range, ~0.7–2.5 μm or 14,000–4,000 cm^{-1}; the mid-infrared (MIR) range, ~2.5–25 μm or 4,000–400 cm^{-1}; and the far-infrared (FIR) range, ~25–1,000 μm or 400–10 cm^{-1}, where the cm^{-1} unit measures the wavenumber, which is the reciprocal of the wavelength. The MIR range is better suited for the study of the fundamental molecular vibrations in a wide range of compounds, both organic and inorganic. The FIR range allows to better detect rotational transitions and some compounds with transition metals, for instance the oxides. This is because the mass of the atoms in the molecular bond that produces the vibration is inversely correlated to the wavenumber, that is, larger chemical species tend to absorb at lower wavenumbers. The NIR range highlights overtones and combined vibrational modes. For these reasons, the MIR is the preferred range to probe the composition of archaeological sediments and materials, where silicates, carbonates, and phosphates are the major mineral classes (van der Marel & Beutelspacher 1976). Therefore, the explanations and examples provided herein are all based on the MIR range.

Molecular vibrations in matter are triggered when the frequency of the incident radiation matches the vibrational frequency of functional groups in molecules, generating a change in the molecular dipole moment. The degree of change in the dipole moment of the molecule, particle size, wavelength, differences in the refractive index of the sample and dispersion medium, and the direction of the vibration with respect to the electric vector of the incident light determine the intensity of the vibration (van der Marel & Beutelspacher 1976). Functional groups are groups of atoms that are responsible for the characteristic chemical reactions of a molecule, for instance, the carbonate moiety (CO_3^{2-}) in calcium carbonate or the phosphate moiety (PO_4^{3-}) in hydroxyapatite. Vibrations can be of different types, called vibrational modes. These are represented by Greek letters depending on the type of molecule and its symmetry species, and include stretching modes (v) and several deformation modes: bending or scissoring (δ), rocking (ρ), wagging (ω), and twisting (τ) (Herzberg 1945). In the case of minerals, most vibrations are labeled with v (Farmer 1974). Vibrations increase the temperature of the material by dissipating as heat. Infrared light is absorbed by different molecules only at specific wavelengths or regions in the spectrum, which results in an infrared spectrum characterized by reduced intensities in the portions where molecules absorb, which are called absorption bands. The ratio of the intensity of the incident light and that of the light transmitted by the sample is called transmittance (T), which is the unit measure of the intensity of absorption and is displayed as a function of wavenumber, varying between 0 and 1. Often, transmittance is multiplied by 100 and shown in $\%T$ units. The $\%T$ unit was commonly used in infrared spectra until recently, although today transmission spectra are displayed in absorbance (A), which is the negative logarithm of the transmittance, and thus a unitless quantity. Similar to $\%T$, when samples are probed using reflected light (see Section 2.4.2), the unit measure is reflectance ($\%R$). In the ATR mode, absorbance is used, but the scale is different compared with the transmission mode due to the different path of the infrared beam through a crystal (Farmer 1974; van der Marel & Beutelspacher 1976; Schrader 1995; Diem 2015; Kaur *et al.* 2021).

Given that different molecules and groups of molecules absorb in specific portions of the infrared spectrum, the position and shape of their absorption bands can be used to determine the nature of the material being analyzed. Therefore, infrared spectroscopy is mainly used as a qualitative method of analysis to determine the composition of a sample. Quantification of phases in single-compound materials and in mixtures is possible, although rather laborious, to the point that X-ray diffraction (XRD) offers a more accurate and rapid option in the case of crystalline phases, including complex mixtures. One way to quantify phases using infrared spectroscopy is to calculate the absorptivity of each band (e.g., Vagenas *et al.* 2003). Alternatively, calibration standards such as single compounds or mixtures of two compounds in known amounts can be prepared and measured to determine changes in band intensity or area caused by changing proportions (e.g., Loftus *et al.* 2015).

2.2 Instrument Setup

Infrared spectrometers include a broad band "black body" light source (generally a hot filament) that generates the infrared beam. Mirrors direct the beam to the interferometer, where the light intensity is divided into two components by a beamsplitter, one that is transmitted and one that is reflected. The transmitted component is redirected to the beamsplitter by a fixed mirror, whereas the reflected component is reflected by a movable mirror (moving back and forth), through which it reaches the beamsplitter again where it is recombined with the other component. Here, half of the light intensity is directed back to the source and half is directed to the sample by a mirror, and from the sample it reaches the detector, usually through another mirror. Detectors are mainly thermal (pyroelectric) of the DTGS (deuterated triglycine sulfate) type. At this stage, there are two light beams propagating to the detector, one generated by the fixed mirror and one generated by the movable mirror. These beams undergo destructive and constructive interference depending on the difference in their paths, which is determined by the position of the movable mirror at any given time. The intensity pattern in the infrared beam produced by the movable mirror, called interferogram, is the signal recorded by the detector (Figure 1). The path difference between the two components of the beam needs to be measured accurately, and for this reason, a reference He-Ne laser beam travels through the interferometer and a separate detector measures the laser intensity variation produced by the interferometer. When the movable mirror moves half the laser wavelength, which in He-Ne lasers is stable and accurately known, the spectrometer software reads the signal from the DTGS detector and records it as a point in the interferogram. The high accuracy of the laser wavelength reference translates into excellent alignment of the repetitive scans of the interferometer and the high accuracy of the wavenumbers. The software then performs a Fourier transform on the interferogram to obtain an infrared spectrum. See Diem (2015) for a detailed description of infrared spectrometers and their theoretical background.

Commercial infrared spectrometers are produced by several brands and come as benchtop (i.e., not movable) or "portable" (movable) instruments. The portable version can be safely transported by car and by plane (cabin only to avoid damage) and used at archaeological excavations, including at cave sites and under conditions of high humidity. Depending on the type of detector,

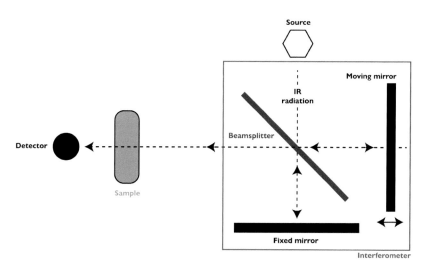

Figure 1 Schematic representation of the main components of an infrared spectrometer.

infrared spectrometers may cover only the MIR range, or they may reach into the NIR and FIR. All spectrometers require dry-air atmosphere to preserve the internal optics from oxidation, avoid deterioration of the potassium bromide (KBr) windows that link the instrument to the sample chamber, and limit noise in the spectra caused by humidity and CO_2. To that end, instruments include a replaceable desiccant (which can be dried in an oven if wet) and also the option to purge the instrument with a dry-air or nitrogen system. In addition, instruments should always be kept on to prevent the accumulation of humidity. Besides the desiccant, infrared spectrometers require little maintenance, such as the verification of the beam alignment by means of a polystyrene standard and the replacement of the light source and KBr windows every ~10 years. Generally, infrared spectrometers are designed in a way that allows to change the sample compartment based on the acquisition mode and the nature of the sample (gas, liquid, or solid), which in turn requires a specific gear for sample preparation (see Section 2.4). Different brands produce their own software to operate the spectrometer and elaborate spectra, for example, to create macros for the swift calculation of band intensity and area ratios.

2.3 Sample Collection

Fourier transform infrared spectroscopy of archaeological sediments starts in the field. The sampling strategy should be devised according to the question(s) driving the research design, and keeping in mind the limitations posed by logistics and available resources. Clearly, an on-site laboratory including an infrared spectrometer allows more rapid and substantial analyses, since spectra are collected in a matter of minutes and samples do not require shipment to the home laboratory (e.g., Weiner 2010; Finkelstein *et al.* 2012). In the absence of such a setup, systematic sampling of all sediments and features might be more convenient if the site is located in a remote area and a second visit is not planned, or in the case of a salvage excavation. On the contrary, targeted sampling is certainly more cost-effective for recurrent fieldwork seasons.

Ideally, samples should be collected from standing sections at the edge of a trench or in witness baulks, if the site is excavated by large squares. This approach allows distinguishing different sedimentary features and layers, whose thickness cannot be assessed by looking at a horizontal surface, which in the end might lead to the mixing of sediments. Often, however, this is not possible at sites excavated by large open areas, where the lateral variability of horizontal surfaces needs to be taken into consideration. Obviously, in this case, samples should be collected from a horizontal surface as soon as it is uncovered and by avoiding trampling. Complex features such as cooking installations, kilns, burials, storage pits, and so on, given their inherent variability, cannot be reduced to general guidelines and should be the object of dedicated sampling strategies in line with the goals of the research.

Sediments should be collected with metal tools, such as trowels and spoons, which allow better control on sediment removal (especially when it is compacted) and prevent contamination in the case of organic materials for radiocarbon dating. These tools are impractical when it comes to thin laminae of powdery substances (e.g., phytoliths, wood ash, organics), which should be collected using small spatulas or tweezers, as in the case of fragile chunks. Sediments can be placed in any type of container, although the choice should be dictated by logistics, storing capacity, and the type of laboratory analysis. Several scientists prefer liquid scintillation vials made of polyethylene because they are small enough for swift storing and shipping and yet they contain enough sediment (20 ml) to allow multiple types of analysis. Bigger vials may be used if large quantities of sediments are required. Zip-lock plastic bags are another viable option, although they tend to break and do not last many years in storage. Glass vials could be used as well; however, besides being significantly more expensive than polyethylene, they increase the overall weight of the samples, which translates into increased shipping costs. In addition, they are more prone to breakage during transport. Nevertheless, glass vials should be considered for samples that are subject to contamination from carbon, such as charcoal for radiocarbon dating. The latter is often stored in aluminum foil folded up in an envelope, which is convenient during fieldwork but may eventually oxidize and break with time and continuous handling. Larger items embedded in sediments, that is, rocks, ceramics, and faunal material, should be collected by hand with the necessary precautions in view of specific laboratory analyses (e.g., DNA, residue analysis, radiocarbon dating), and stored accordingly. Regardless of the storage medium, all containers should be labeled following the numbering system relevant to the fieldwork project and in a manner that prevents fading of the ink. Labels written with an indelible marker on masking tape wrapped around vials seem to be durable; plastic-lined stickers add protection from liquids. Eventually, after several fieldwork seasons, these efforts will lead to the establishment of a sediment library that documents the stratigraphic sequence of the site.

2.4 Acquisition Modes and Sample Preparation

Samples may be analyzed using three acquisition modes: transmission, reflectance, and photoacoustic. In transmission, the sample is suspended in a pellet made from a medium that does not absorb infrared radiation in the MIR, such as

KBr or potassium chloride (KCl). The infrared beam travels through the pellet, and the portion that is not absorbed reaches the detector, from which it is converted into a spectrum showing the absorption bands of the molecules in the sample. In reflectance, the infrared beam impinges on the sample, and the detector collects the reflected component. This can be achieved in different ways, called total reflectance, ATR, and diffuse reflectance (DRIFT). In total reflectance, the instrument collects the entire reflected component of the infrared beam. In ATR, the instrument collects the component of the infrared beam that is reflected as an evanescent wave through a crystal in contact with the sample. In DRIFT, the instrument collects the component of the infrared beam reflected by a powdered sample mixed with KBr placed in a cup holder. In photoacoustic spectroscopy (PAS), the sample absorbs modulated infrared light and produces thermal waves that in turn generate acoustic waves through a carrier gas inside an enclosed cell, which are detected by a microphone or a cantilever.

These acquisition modes require specific sample preparation procedures, which are described in Sections 2.4.1 and 2.4.2. Given the limited archaeological applications of DRIFT and PAS in MIR spectroscopy (e.g., Angelini & Bellintani 2005; Stevenson *et al.* 2013), these methods are not discussed any further. All reference spectra of standard materials included here are provided in transmission and ATR modes.

2.4.1 Transmission

To obtain transmission infrared spectra, it is first necessary to suspend the sample in a pellet made of KBr (Stimson & O'Donnell 1952). The gear for pellet preparation includes FTIR-grade KBr, a mortar and pestle made of agate or porcelain, a pellet die, a metal spatula with cup holder to transfer sample from the vial to the mortar, a similar spatula to transfer KBr from its container to the mortar, weighing paper to transfer the sample–KBr mixture from the mortar to the pellet die, paper wipes for cleaning, a pellet press (handheld or benchtop), and a ceramic lamp with infrared reflector bulb (at least 250 W) to keep KBr and sample dry (Figure 2). Coarse-grained KBr tends to be less hygroscopic because of the smaller amount of surface area exposed to air. It is advisable to place all the tools near the heat lamp to keep them dry. Pellet preparation is shown in Video 1.

A small amount of sample, typically 5 mg or less, is transferred to the mortar using the spatula to avoid inadvertently sorting grains, and ground to a fine powder using the pestle. The particle size of this powder is not fixed, although a rule of thumb is to stop grinding when grit is no longer felt between

Figure 2 Heat lamp and reflector bulb with KBr vial, agate mortar and pestle, and spatulas.

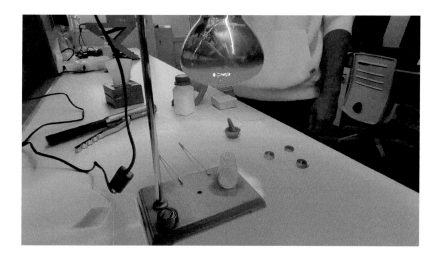

Video 1 Sample preparation for transmission mode. Video files available at
www.cambridge/toffolo

the mortar and the pestle. This operation is not only meant to facilitate sample suspension in KBr but also to homogenize the many components in the sample, thus making it representative of a certain sediment layer, feature, or material. In addition, reducing particle size allows decreasing the loss of radiation caused by the reflection of the infrared beam onto large particles. Loose sediments can be easily crushed provided that large pebbles are removed prior to grinding (also to avoid overrepresentation of components that might be minor ones or that can be analyzed separately), whereas larger fragments such as rocks, plasters, ceramics, teeth, and bones require greater effort, especially when the latter contain collagen. After grinding, all excess material is removed with a wipe to avoid overloading of the infrared spectrum, which results in "broken" bands for high absorbance values (Figure 3). After that, a few mg of KBr are added to the mortar and ground with the sample using the pestle. The amount of KBr varies depending on the diameter and thickness of the pellet die. For pellets with a diameter of 7 mm, ~20–40 mg of KBr are sufficient depending on the thickness of the die. Larger diameters require greater quantities of KBr to prevent pellet failure upon pressing. The mixture is then transferred to the pellet die using weighing paper, and pressed. Benchtop presses include a gauge that helps quantifying the amount of pressure necessary to obtain a pellet. Usually, 2 tons suffice for 7-mm pellets. Some hand presses allow a rough, indirect measure of the exerted pressure based on the degree of tightening of the screw that holds the die set in place when pressed with the piston. This method requires some practice to become accustomed to it and avoid breakage of the press, but it is slightly faster than a benchtop press. The resulting pellet should appear transparent with the suspended sample clearly visible. If the pellet is not well pressed, or too thick, it may be opaque, and this translates into a sloping spectrum baseline

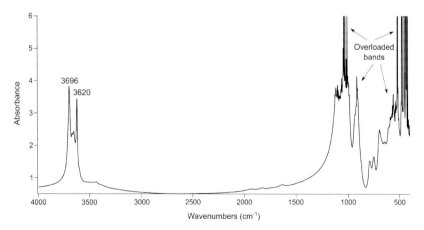

Figure 3 Overloaded spectrum of kaolinite. Note the high absorbance value that translates into "broken" bands under 1,200 cm^{-1}.

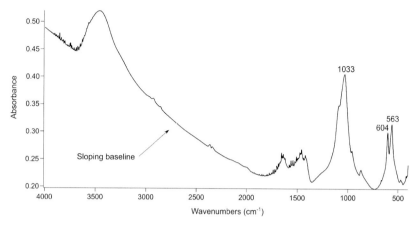

Figure 4 Spectrum of carbonate hydroxyapatite in enamel characterized by a sloping baseline. Note the low absorbance value that translates into a sloping baseline.

in the region 4,000–2,000 cm^{-1}, which may affect spectrum interpretation. This happens also when the quantity of sample is too small or the sample is inherently opaque (e.g., charcoal, iron oxides) (Figure 4). If the pellet is highly reflective, either due to the nature of the sample or to insufficient pressing, the resulting spectrum will appear as a corrugated line, instead of a smooth line (Weiner 2010) (Figure 5).

In the case of samples that need to be repeatedly ground to produce a grinding curve (see Section 2.6.2), the pellet should be lightly ground for the first measurement. After analysis, the pellet is removed from the die, and about half of it is discarded. This is done because the second grinding reduces particle size and thus increases the number of particles that absorb the infrared beam, which may translate into an overloaded spectrum. The remaining half is ground more vigorously, then ~10–20 mg (depending on the required thickness) of KBr are added to replace the discarded material and mixed, and the resulting powder is pressed into a pellet (Video 2). This operation is repeated three or more times, depending on the type of material, taking care to increase the strength of the grinding prior to each analysis. For the sake of consistency, the same operator should repeat the grindings. It is important not to grind together the half pellet and the additional KBr, which otherwise will produce a larger volume of fine powder that might result in an opaque pellet, and ultimately in a sloping baseline that is unsuitable for the calculation of band intensity ratios.

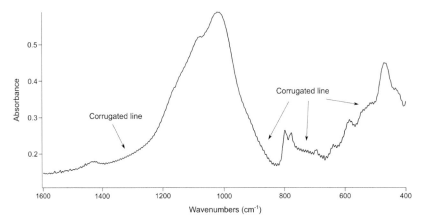

Figure 5 Spectrum of hornfels (metamorphic silicate rock) showing a corrugated line.

Video 2 Repeated pellet grinding for the grinding curve method. Video files available at www.cambridge/toffolo

To avoid contamination, it is important to clean the tools between samples. Similarly, weighing paper should be replaced. The cleaning routine includes washing the mortar and pestle with 1 M HCl to remove carbonates, rinsing with deionized water, and drying with paper or under the heat lamp with the aid of a few drops of acetone, which can also break down some organic molecules (Video 3). The sample spatula and pellet die set should be rubbed with a paper wipe dampened with deionized water, especially when residues of KBr stick to the inner wall of the die.

Video 3 Mortar cleaning procedure. Video files available at www.cambridge/toffolo

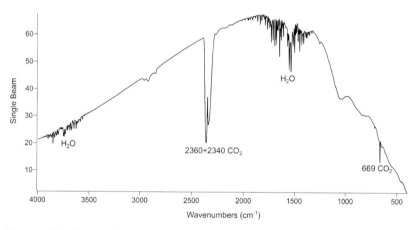

Figure 6 Background transmission spectrum showing the location of water and carbon dioxide bands.

Prior to pellet analysis, it is necessary to collect a background spectrum in the empty sample chamber of the instrument to subtract the contribution of ambient humidity and carbon dioxide (CO_2) from the sample spectrum (Figure 6). Depending on the composition of the atmosphere in the room and within the optical bench, the background spectrum should be collected at regular intervals. The presence of bands at ~2,360, ~2,340, and ~669 cm^{-1} in the sample spectrum indicates that there is too much CO_2 in the room. Transmission analysis is usually performed in the 4,000–400 cm^{-1} (MIR) spectral range, although some benchtop instruments span from 7,500 (NIR) to 250 cm^{-1} (FIR). Spectral resolution may be adjusted based on the nature of the sample and on the research question; a value of 4 cm^{-1} is considered an adequate compromise for most phases and mixtures of phases. The pellet is analyzed in a number of scans that are averaged to obtain the final spectrum; this number can be modified as needed. All settings should be thoroughly reported in publications. The entire process of pellet preparation and analysis takes less than five minutes.

2.4.2 Reflectance

Acquiring infrared spectra in reflectance mode requires less sample preparation compared to transmission (Rubens & Nichols 1897). In total reflectance (or reflection), the sample is simply placed in front of the instrument, at a convenient distance and angle. The background spectrum is collected on a gold plate, which reflects the entirety of the beam. This acquisition mode is not applied to archaeological sediments, except when using an FTIR microscope (see Section 2.5). In ATR, the sample is placed on a stage in contact with a crystal of high refractive index, such as diamond, germanium, silicon, zinc selenide, or zinc sulfide (Fahrenfort 1961; Kaur *et al.* 2021). Benchtop and portable instruments may be equipped with an ATR attachment to the main sample chamber that features a clamp, which presses the sample against the crystal. The infrared beam travels through the crystal and reflects within its inner surface, generating an evanescent wave that penetrates into the sample by a few micrometers. The background spectrum is collected without sample (Figure 7). In this configuration, excellent contact between the crystal and sample is key to obtaining useful spectra. Therefore, flat contact surfaces are

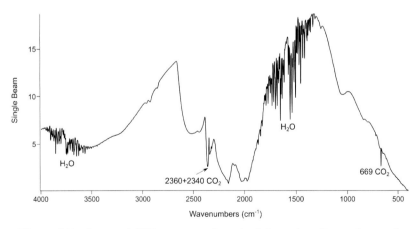

Figure 7 Background ATR spectrum (acquired through a diamond crystal) showing the location of water and carbon dioxide bands. Note the large difference in values of the *y*-axis scale compared with transmission.

Video 4 Sample preparation for ATR mode. Video files available at
www.cambridge/toffolo

privileged when analyzing samples that cannot be pulverized (e.g., bones, stone tools). Alternatively, samples may be ground to a fine powder following the same procedure as for transmission spectra, and pressed against the ATR crystal (Video 4). Polished slabs and thin sections are inherently flat but may require additional, fine-grained polishing. In both total reflectance and ATR, the instrument detector collects the reflected component. In reflectance, spectra are displayed in %R units, which measure the intensity of the bands, whereas in ATR, the spectra are displayed in absorbance. The general considerations about spectral range, spectral resolution, and number of scans described for transmission apply to reflectance as well. A major difference between transmission and ATR spectra is that bands under 2,000 cm^{-1} may be located at lower wavenumbers and may be characterized by a different intensity and shape compared to transmission. This depends on the refractive index of the ATR crystal and that of the sample, and on the angle of incidence of the infrared beam within the crystal. The FTIR software usually includes an ATR correction tool that allows to correct for these distortions and thus makes ATR spectra more easily comparable to transmission spectra, although the two never coincide (e.g., Calandra *et al.* 2022). This is likely due to the fact that the contact between ATR crystal and sample powder is not perfect and changes each time the sample is removed and replaced in contact, and that sediments are mixtures of phases characterized by several different refractive indices.

2.5 Infrared Microspectroscopy

Fourier transform infrared microscopes are instruments that combine the capabilities of optical microscopes and FTIR spectrometers (Berna 2017). Therefore, they allow the analysis of spatially resolved samples in transmission, reflection, and ATR modes, with clear benefits for the analysis of archaeological sediments within their original depositional context (Goldberg & Berna 2010). Fourier transform infrared microspectroscopy gained momentum in the 1980s after the introduction of computer-aided Fourier transform processing and advancements in IR detector technology (Messerschmidt & Harthcock 1988; Derrick *et al.* 1999).

The combination between FTIR spectrometer and optical microscope is based on the layout of the nosepiece, which features both optical objectives and infrared light condensers. Most FTIR microscopes can also be equipped with an analyzer and polarizer that allow the observation of samples in cross-polarized light, necessary to determine the interference colors of crystalline phases. The latest instrument setups include an integrated light source, making them independent from attached spectrometers. Regions of interest (ROIs) in the sample can be located manually through the optical objective using an eyepiece and stage knobs, or through a software-operated automated stage and camera, which collects mosaics of scans. The selected ROIs are then analyzed with a specific aperture size of the infrared beam using the FTIR objectives, which in recent models coincide with the optical objectives. This configuration makes it possible to collect spectra while viewing the sample, even while adjusting the position in order to achieve the best results. In transmission mode, the infrared beam travels through the objective and the sample where it is focused by the condenser, and the remaining component is directed toward the detector. In reflection mode, the beam travels through the objective and the reflected component travels back to the detector through the same objective. The same principle applies to ATR, with the difference that before and after reaching the sample, the beam is reflected within a crystal characterized by a high refractive index, usually germanium or diamond (Humecki 1995; Diem 2015). The extent of the MIR spectral range that can be probed depends on the detector. Deuterated triglycine sulfate (room temperature) detectors allow analyses within the $4,000–400$ cm^{-1} range but require relatively longer collection times (~2 minutes for sixty-four scans) and are more subject to noise. Mercury cadmium telluride (MCT) detectors are semiconductor materials that allow shorter acquisition times (less than thirty seconds for sixty-four scans) and produce less noise. However, they need to be cooled with liquid nitrogen and may be limited to $4,000–675$ cm^{-1}. Linear array detectors, also cooled with liquid nitrogen, are the most rapid but are limited to $4,000–715$ cm^{-1}. On the other hand, they allow fast chemical imaging of a sample. Therefore, one needs to find the best tradeoff between the speed of measurement and spectral range depending on the research question. For instance, information on the heat alteration of carbonate hydroxyapatite in bones based on the occurrence of the band at ~630 cm^{-1} can only be obtained with a DTGS or MCT-B detector. Typically, the best spatial resolution that can be achieved is ~20 μm, although instruments connected to a synchrotron light source can reach a spatial resolution of ~1 μm (Miller & Dumas 2006). Background spectra are collected in the same manner described in Sections 2.4.1 and 2.4.2 for regular FTIR spectrometers. Spectral resolution, number of scans, aperture size of the infrared beam, and other options can be modified based on research goals.

Depending on the instrument setup, samples may be analyzed in gas, liquid, and solid forms (Diem 2015). The most common types of samples for archaeological applications are powders and particles embedded in barium fluoride pellets, micromorphology and petrographic thin sections (30-μm thickness), and polished slabs (Berna 2017). Thin sections may be analyzed in all acquisition modes provided that they are not covered, whereas polished slabs only allow reflection and ATR due to their thickness. In transmission mode, the glass slide on which the thin section is mounted exhibits strong absorptions below ~2,400 cm^{-1}, which makes it useful only for phases characterized by absorption bands at higher wavenumbers, for example, clay minerals (Berna & Goldberg 2008). In addition, both thin sections and polished slabs of unconsolidated materials show the absorption bands of the mounting medium (polyester or epoxy), which are located at ~2,900 cm^{-1} (Figure 8). In reflection and ATR modes, the acquisition of spectra is affected by light scattering, which may require additional fine-grit polishing of the thin sections (down to 1 μm depending on the instrument) in order to reduce noise. Bands of polyester and epoxy are also visible below 2,000 cm^{-1}.

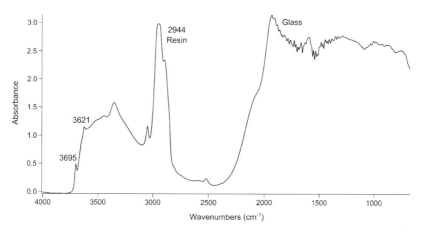

Figure 8 Transmission spectrum of clay minerals (bands at 3,695 and 3,621 cm^{-1}) in thin section, showing the location of the resin and glass absorptions.

2.6 Extracting Information from Infrared Spectra

The operational steps described in Section 2.4 can be learned in a matter of a few hours. The main obstacle presents itself after analysis, when interpreting spectra. An automatic search through spectral libraries can be useful in the case of a single phase represented in the spectrum, but that is seldom the case with archaeological sediments. Multi-phase mixtures are not correctly identified by the search tools currently available in the FTIR software due to complex overlaying of bands characteristic of different phases, unless the same mixture is already present in the library. Even when algorithms are developed to encompass all the subtleties of band shift and broadening, they are really effective with single phases (e.g., Chowdhury *et al.* 2021). This is bound to change in the future, but for the time being the best approach is to learn how to recognize the key phases of archaeological relevance one by one, how they change when they are exposed to elevated temperatures or undergo diagenesis, and how they appear when they are mixed. However, before delving into the description of specific components, it is important to know how information can be extracted from infrared spectra, besides the identification of phases.

2.6.1 Band Shift, Intensity, and Broadening

As stated, the bands in the infrared spectrum result from the interaction between infrared light and molecules, and the ways the latter vibrate. Specific molecules produce infrared bands at specific locations and with specific intensities and shapes. Therefore, phase identification is based on the occurrence of specific sets of bands, which tend to occur at the same location in the spectrum. In fact, band locations in transmission spectra may change by about ± 1 cm^{-1} upon repeated measurement of the same pellet. This makes FTIR spectroscopy remarkably reproducible. In ATR mode, this deviation may be somewhat larger if the sample powder is displaced from the holder, presumably because the reflected component of the beam never travels from particle to particle following the same path. Another consequence of using ATR (and reflectance) is that band locations may shift compared to transmission, and this should be kept in mind when comparing spectra acquired in different modes. Let us consider the spectrum of calcium carbonate ($CaCO_3$) in the form of calcite as example. In transmission, calcite spar exhibits three main bands at ~1,420 (v_3), ~875 (v_2), and ~712 (v_4) cm^{-1}. The v_3 has the highest intensity, followed by the v_2 and v_4. In ATR, the same bands are located at ~1,393, ~873, and ~712 cm^{-1}, respectively, and both the v_2 and v_4 show higher intensity relative to the v_3 compared with transmission (Figure 9). Depending on the acquisition mode, the three main bands of calcite always appear at the same location, and the occurrence of

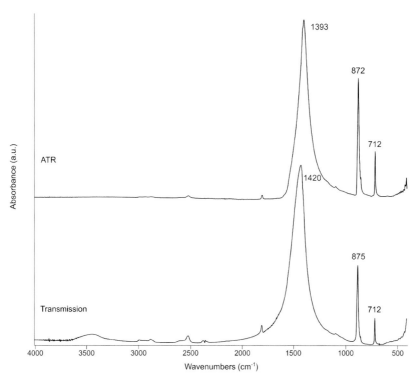

Figure 9 Transmission and ATR spectra of calcite spar. Note that bands exhibit different shape, intensity, and position in the two modes (a.u.: arbitrary units). For instance, the v_3 in the ATR spectrum is more asymmetric and narrower compared to the transmission spectrum; the v_2 and v_4 have higher intensity relative to the v_3 in the ATR spectrum than in the transmission spectrum.

this set of bands is required for correct phase identification. However, these absorptions are influenced by the different manners in which the C–O bonds of the carbonate functional group interact with infrared radiation. For that reason, small shifts in band position should be regarded as potentially informative because they are caused by variations in the molecular arrangement or composition of the phase. For instance, when calcite contains small amounts of magnesium carbonate, as in magnesian calcite, the v_4 shifts to slightly higher wavenumbers, up to 717 cm^{-1} for 13 mol% Mg content (Wang *et al.* 1997). The v_2 and v_4 of calcite are subject to shifts of ~–1.5 cm^{-1} when heated to temperatures around 600 K (Xu & Poduska 2014). Band shifts can also occur as a result of phase transitions. Aragonite, a metastable polymorph of $CaCO_3$ at ambient conditions, exhibits bands at ~1,475 (v_3), ~856 (v_2), and ~713 + 700 (v_4) cm^{-1}. It is the same compound as calcite, but with different spatial arrangement of the carbonate groups, hence the different band locations. When heated to temperatures above 300 °C, aragonite reorganizes its atoms to take the structure of calcite, with a consequent shift of the three main bands to the calcite locations (Toffolo 2021 and references therein). Another effect of heat is the decrease in intensity of some bands, for instance the v_4 of calcite (Xu & Poduska 2014). Similar changes in band location and intensity affect other phases exposed to elevated temperatures, such as clay minerals and cryptocrystalline quartz (Berna *et al.* 2007; Schmidt & Frölich 2011; Weiner *et al.* 2015).

In general, broad overlapping bands in the spectra of archaeological sediments are characteristic of organic macromolecules, whereas sharp bands are produced by minerals, especially in the region below 900 cm^{-1} (Weiner 2010). Changes in the full width at half maximum (FWHM) of the bands, either by broadening or narrowing, can have multiple causes. Small particle sizes translate into narrow bands, whereas large particles of the same phase produce broad bands (Duyckaerts 1959). The degree of short-range atomic order of the phase also affects the FWHM. Poorly ordered crystals and amorphous phases result in broad bands, opposite to well-ordered crystals, which produce narrow bands (Addadi *et al.* 2003; Gueta *et al.* 2006). These two trends often work in opposite ways in the same phase, which makes it difficult to determine whether it is well ordered or exhibits relatively small crystals. The grinding curve method (see Section 2.6.2) was developed to decouple these effects. Broadening can also occur as a consequence of intensity decrease caused by elevated temperatures, as in the v_4 of calcite, which in turn is linked to an increase in lattice defects that make the crystal poorly ordered (Xu & Poduska 2014). In other instances, such as carbonate hydroxyapatite in bone, exposure to high temperature increases the degree of atomic order of crystals (Shipman *et al.* 1984).

2.6.2 Band Intensity Ratios

Given that any change in the molecular arrangement of a phase may determine changes in the shape, width, intensity, and position of bands, these in turn can provide information regarding the proportions of specific functional groups, and the degree of crystallinity of minerals. Crystallinity is broadly defined as periodic order in three dimensions at the atomic level, and here crystallinity is referred to in terms of crystallite size and density of defects in the crystal structure. Different formation paths introduce distinct densities of structural defects, which affect the degree of crystallinity. In calcite, Iceland spar is characterized by single periodic order across macroscopic distances, whereas amorphous calcium carbonate (ACC) exhibits short-range order but no periodicity at the long scale (Addadi *et al.* 2003).

Information is often extracted from infrared spectra by calculating the ratio of the intensity of bands that are representative of specific molecules, or that are directly affected by distinct densities of structural defects in the crystal lattice. To calculate intensity in a standardized manner, a baseline should be drawn to mark the limit of the band area, usually connecting the minima of the troughs at either side of the band. For instance, the CO_3^{2-} bands of carbonate hydroxyapatite at ~1,540 (type A) and ~1,415 (type B) cm^{-1} can be divided by the PO_4^3 band at ~603 cm^{-1} (or the PO_4^{3-} band at ~1,035 cm^{-1}) to obtain the proportion of carbonates to phosphates in bone and tooth enamel, with higher ratios indicative of diagenetic alteration (e.g., Featherstone *et al.* 1984; Wright & Schwarcz 1996; Sponheimer & Lee-Thorp 1999), although Trueman *et al.* (2004) found that the carbonate content might be overestimated if organic material is present in the bone, as it produces an absorption that is overlaid on the ~1,415 cm^{-1} band. Other similar ratios can help characterize the proportions of calcite and collagen in archaeological bone (see Section 3.3.1). The phosphate v_4 band, represented by the doublet at ~603 and ~567 cm^{-1}, can be used as an indicator of crystallinity of bone mineral. The extent of splitting of these peaks is low in fresh carbonate hydroxyapatite minerals, which are poorly ordered. Upon recrystallization, by diagenesis or exposure to elevated temperatures, crystals become more ordered and the splitting of the doublet becomes more pronounced. The degree of separation of the peaks is calculated by dividing the sum of their intensities by the intensity of the valley between them (Figure 10). This infrared splitting factor (IRSF) allows determining the state of preservation of bones, dentine, and tooth enamel, although it cannot

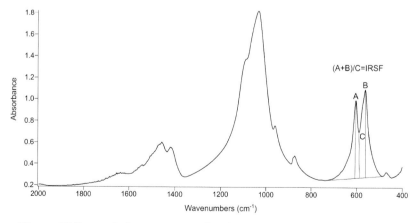

Figure 10 Transmission spectrum of carbonate hydroxyapatite in enamel, showing the location of the bands used in the calculation of the IRSF. A: 603 cm^{-1}; B: 567 cm^{-1}.

separate the opposite effects of particle size and short-range atomic order (Termine & Posner 1966; Weiner & Bar-Yosef 1990; Stiner *et al.* 1995).

Since the degree of crystallinity is strongly related to the formation path of the mineral, in some cases it is possible to distinguish different formation mechanisms, some of which are of archaeological importance (Weiner 2010). Taking again calcite as example, Beniash *et al.* (1997) found that the ratio of the intensity of the v_2 and v_4 in transmission reflects the degree of crystallinity of calcite in sea urchin larval spicules, with higher ratios (>6) characteristic of the early stages of formation of the spicules when calcite is poorly ordered, whereas calcite spar shows values around 3. This phenomenon is caused by the weak intensity of the v_4 in poorly ordered calcite, where this band is more affected by atomic disorder compared to the v_2 (Gueta *et al.* 2006). The same trend was observed by Chu *et al.* (2008) in experimental and archaeological wood ash and lime plaster. Values around 4 are typical of wood ash, whereas lime plaster shows ratios around 6; archaeological plasters are characterized by values ranging from 3 to 6, indicating different degrees of recrystallization, in which poorly ordered calcite in fresh plaster dissolves and reprecipitates as more ordered crystals that produce higher v_4 bands. However, the authors observed that results are reproducible only in spectra where the FWHM of the v_3 falls between 110 and 130 cm^{-1}. This limitation is caused by the particle size effect mentioned in Section 2.6.1, whereby larger particles (with FWHM >130 cm^{-1}) produce broader bands that are not representative of lattice defects caused by exposure to fire. This problem was solved with the development of the grinding curve method.

Grinding Curves

The opposite effects of particle-size-dependent optical absorption and atomic order on the shape of infrared spectra of calcite were noted when calculating the v_2/v_4 ratio outside of a specific range of FWHM of the v_3. This prompted the investigation of the behavior of the v_3, which becomes significantly narrower with increased grinding of the sample as the v_2/v_4 ratio increases (Figure 11). It was found that upon repeated grinding of the same KBr pellet, the intensity of the v_2 and v_4 absorptions, normalized to the intensity of the v_3 absorption for easier comparison of pellets from different grindings, decreases. At the same time, bands become narrower. This is caused by increasing band sharpening and absorbance as a result of decreasing particle size, which affects the v_3 much more than the other two bands. By plotting the normalized intensity of the v_2 and v_4 absorptions for each grinding, a trendline ("grinding curve") is obtained, which allows to monitor atomic order independently from particle size. In fact, the application of this procedure to different types of calcite, including Iceland

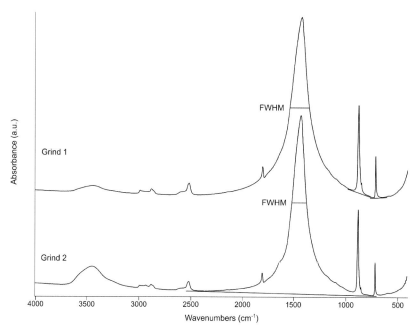

Figure 11 Spectra of calcite showing the decrease in FWHM values upon repeated grinding, and the baselines used for the calculation of band intensity (a.u.: arbitrary units).

spar, limestone, chalk, wood ash, and lime plaster, produced distinct grinding curves for each of these materials (Regev *et al.* 2010a) (Figure 12). Poduska *et al.* (2011) showed that the shape of each grinding curve is determined by changes in absorption caused by different particle sizes, whereas the offset of a curve (relative to a simulated ideal curve) depends on the degree of short-range atomic order of crystals. Curves showing more pronounced slope are characteristic of poorly ordered calcite, such as lime plaster, as a result of the inherently lower v_4 intensity observed in pyrogenic materials (Chu *et al.* 2008). The advantage of this method is that it can decouple the effects of particle-size-dependent optical absorption and atomic order on band shape, thus making analysis independent of the degree of grinding of the sample. Therefore, grinding curves can be used as reference to determine whether calcite found at archaeological sites formed through geogenic processes, biomineralization, or pyrotechnological activities related to human occupation. Similar reference curves have been established for aragonite (Suzuki *et al.* 2011; Toffolo *et al.* 2019a) and carbonate hydroxyapatite (Asscher *et al.* 2011b; Dal Sasso *et al.* 2018). It is advisable to establish grinding curves using standard materials from

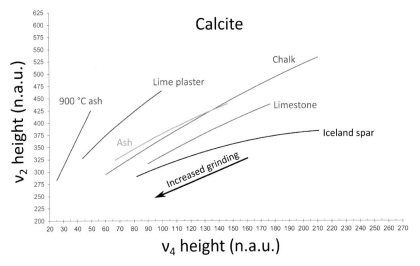

Figure 12 Grinding curves of calcite, reprinted from *Journal of Archaeological Science*, 37(12), Regev *et al.* (2010a: Figure 7), with permission from Elsevier (n.a.u.: normalized absorbance units).

the surroundings of an archaeological site (e.g., local limestone for calcite, specific taxa for carbonate hydroxyapatite), as they may exhibit different degrees of atomic order compared to published references from other regions. Since grinding curves are obtained by analyzing samples in transmission, it is not possible to use them as reference for spectra acquired in ATR or reflectance.

2.6.3 Chemical Maps

Besides single spectra, some FTIR microscopes offer the possibility to convert the output into a chemical map, which is a mosaic of camera scans of a ROI overlaid by colors representing the different phases detected in the spectra, accompanied by a list of the identified phases and their percentage (Figure 13). Phase identification is based on an automated search through a reference library, which in the case of archaeological sediments needs to be developed since free databases are not available. Depending on the software, the search can be tailored to a specific band or set of bands, or it can be extended to the entire spectral range. In addition, a threshold may be entered to define what a correct match is. For instance, a 75 percent match between library and sample spectra is considered sufficient to correctly identify a phase (e.g., Toffolo *et al.* 2020a, 2023b). In the absence of a reference library, which obviously should include transmission, reflection, and ATR spectra of the same phase in order to fully

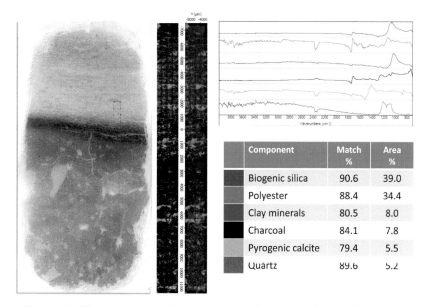

Component	Match %	Area %
Biogenic silica	90.6	39.0
Polyester	88.4	34.4
Clay minerals	80.5	8.0
Charcoal	84.1	7.8
Pyrogenic calcite	79.4	5.5
Quartz	89.6	5.2

Figure 13 Chemical map of a transect in a micromorphology thin section, reprinted from *Archaeological and Anthropological Sciences*, 15, Toffolo *et al.* (2023b: figure 9), with permission from SNCSC.

exploit the chemical map output, intensity maps may help identify phases by highlighting with different colors the areas where a specific band exhibits more absorbance (or %R) compared to other bands (e.g., Ogloblin Ramírez *et al.* 2023). For example, ROIs characterized by bands of clay minerals between 4,000 and 3,400 cm^{-1} will appear blue (high intensity) in the map, whereas ROI devoid of clay minerals will appear red (low intensity).

3 Infrared Spectra of the Main Components of Archaeological Sediments

Training one's eye in the interpretation of infrared spectra requires time and an understanding of how different phases may interact with one another and when exposed to elevated temperatures and/or groundwater, which in turn is based on knowledge of their physical and chemical properties. One important aspect to keep in mind is that infrared spectra are additive: when the bands of two different phases overlap, they appear overlaid, with the less intense band appearing as a shoulder of the other one (Weiner 2010: figure 12.1). When the two bands also have similar intensity, for example, the ~525 cm^{-1} band of montmorillonite and the ~512 cm^{-1} band of quartz, the resulting band will be located between the two, around 519 cm^{-1} (see Mixtures, Supplementary Material). The following sections illustrate the spectra of the main components found in archaeological sediments and their interpretation. Spectra were collected using a Thermo Scientific Nicolet iS5 spectrometer equipped with an iD1 transmission compartment in the 4,000–400 cm^{-1} range at 4 cm^{-1} resolution, and in thirty-two scans. Spectra were collected with the same instrument and settings in ATR mode using an iD7 ATR diamond crystal compartment, and are available in figures in the Supplementary Material. Nomenclature about IR-active vibrations can be found in Farmer (1974), van der Marel and Beutelspacher (1976), Lin-Vien *et al.* (1991), and Chukanov (2014). Freely available spectral libraries include those of the Kimmel Center for Archaeological Science (transmission; https://centers.weizmann.ac.il/kimmel-arch/infrared-spectra-library), the RRUFF Project database (ATR; https://rruff .info/), and the IRUG database (transmission; http://www.irug.org/). The spectra included in here, both transmission and ATR, are available in the Supplementary Material and in Zenodo (https://doi.org/10.5281/zenodo.14170891), and report the source locality or manufacturer where available. In the following spectra, loosely absorbed water molecules are represented by a broad band around ~3,400 cm^{-1} (O–H stretching) and a shallow band at ~1,630 cm^{-1} (O–H bending).

3.1 Silicates

Silicates are by far the most common component at archaeological sites across the globe. They are characterized by a main band at ~1,000 cm^{-1} and shallower bands under 800 cm^{-1}, which can be more or less broad based on the degree of crystallinity of the phase and its particle size (Asscher *et al.* 2017).

3.1.1 Phyllosilicates

Phyllosilicates include clay minerals, micas, chlorites, and serpentine (Table 1). The clay minerals are almost ubiquitous in archaeological sediments, as well as in architectural materials and ceramics, and comprise the kaolinite and smectite

Table 1 Phyllosilicates and their chemical formula.

Phyllosilicate mineral	Chemical formula
Kaolinite	$Al_2Si_2O_5(OH)_4$
Montmorillonite	$(Na,Ca)(Al,Mg)_2(Si_4O_{10})(OH)_2 \cdot nH_2O$
Illite	$(K,H_3O)(Al,Mg,Fe)_2(Si,Al)_4O_{10}[(OH)_2,(H_2O)]$
Muscovite	$KAl_2(AlSi_3O_{10})(F,OH)_2$
Biotite	$K(Mg,Fe)_3(AlSi_3O_{10})(F,OH)_2$
Serpentine	$(Mg,Al,Fe)_3Si_2O_5(OH)_4$
Chlorite	$(Mg,Fe)_3(Si,Al)_4O_{10}(OH)_2 \cdot (Mg,Fe)_3(OH)_6$

major groups. Except for illite, all other phyllosilicates are less commonly found in archaeological sediments. For instance, micas may be found in some alluvial deposits and in sediments on top of intrusive igneous rocks (e.g., Birkenfeld *et al.* 2020). The clay mineral groups exhibit shallow bands in the region between 4,000 and 3,500 cm^{-1} (Mg, Al–O–H stretching) a main broad band between ~1,045 and ~1,000 cm^{-1} (Si–O–Si stretching) with shallower bands between 1,100 and 900 cm^{-1} (Si–O, Si–O–Al, Al–O–H stretching), and several bands under ~800 cm^{-1} (Si–O–Al and Si–O bending). However, with few exceptions, clay minerals occur as mixtures in archaeological contexts, and therefore identifying with certainty all the phases in a sediment sample is not possible. The issue is further compounded by the fact that minor differences in ion content, which are to be expected in standard reference materials from different localities, result in subtle changes in the spectrum (van der Marel & Beutelspacher 1976; Madejová 2003). Nonetheless, a few key bands aid in the assessment of the clay mineral groups. Kaolinite, the main mineral in the kaolinite group, exhibits diagnostic bands at ~3,695, ~3,620, ~1,034, ~1,010, ~914, ~541, and ~471 cm^{-1}; montmorillonite, the main mineral in the smectite group, shows diagnostic bands at ~3,630, ~3,425, ~1,045 (with sodium ions), ~1,033 (with calcium ions), ~525, and ~470 cm^{-1} (Figure 14). With regard to micas, illite is characterized by bands similar to those that occur in smectites, and in fact the two groups are often interstratified in sediments; muscovite exhibits prominent bands at ~3,629, ~1,026, ~534, and ~477 cm^{-1}, whereas biotite is characterized by only two major bands located at ~1,000 and ~465 cm^{-1}. Serpentine includes diagnostic bands at ~3,683, ~957, ~622, and ~442 cm^{-1}. Chlorite exhibits a broad band centered at ~3,500 cm^{-1} and prominent bands at ~992 and ~690 cm^{-1} (Figure 15). All phyllosilicates exhibit slightly shifted bands in ATR spectra, and especially the main Si–O–Si band in montmorillonite, which shifts toward ~990 cm^{-1} (Supplementary Material).

Clay minerals are affected by exposure to elevated temperatures and to groundwater rich in foreign ions, which cause structural changes that can be detected in the spectrum. Dehydroxylation and the loss of structurally bound water between 400 and 500 °C cause the decrease in intensity of the bands in the 4,000–3,000 cm^{-1} region, which merge into a shoulder, and the disappearance of the bands at 912 and 525 cm^{-1}, as well as the shift of the main Si–O–Si band toward higher wavenumbers; above 500 °C, the shoulder in the 4,000–3,500 cm^{-1} region eventually disappears, and the Si–O–Si band shifts more, reaching up to 1,084 cm^{-1} at 900 °C and depending on the mixture of clay minerals (Farmer 1974; van der Marel & Beutelspacher 1976; Shoval 1993, 1994; Karkanas *et al.* 2004; Berna *et al.* 2007; Aldeias *et al.* 2016; Karkanas 2021) (Figure 16). Similar band shifts occur when clay minerals lose their

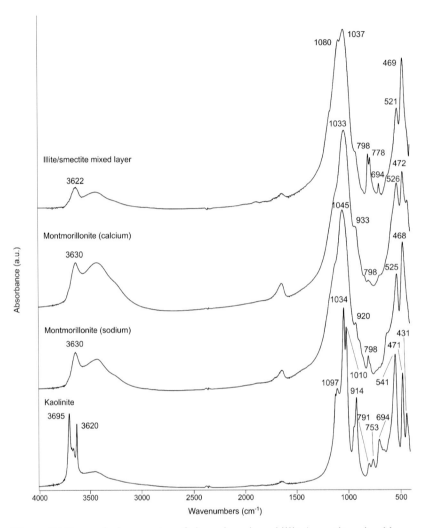

Figure 14 Transmission spectra of clay minerals and illite/smectite mixed layer (a.u.: arbitrary units). The bands at 1,080, 798, 778, and 694 cm^{-1} belong to quartz (see Figure 18).

original structure upon reacting with phosphate ions and water during dia-genesis, and thus other lines of evidence are required to exclude alteration from heat (Weiner *et al.* 2002). Forget *et al.* (2015) observed that the degree of shifting of the Si–O–Si band is not the same when clay minerals are heated in oxidizing or reducing conditions, and thus proposed to measure the FWHM of that band and plot it against the shift in order to distinguish heating temperatures under different heating atmospheres. Since mixtures of clay

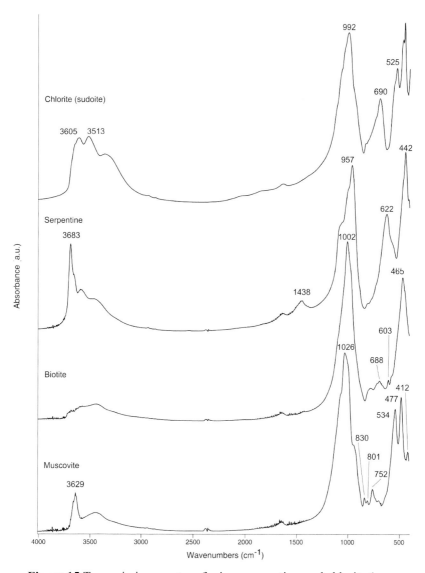

Figure 15 Transmission spectra of micas, serpentine, and chlorite (a.u.: arbitrary units). Note that chlorites represent a large group of phyllosilicates; sudoite is a variety rich in Mg, Al, and Fe.

minerals may be site specific, heating experiments of local natural sediments to create a reference FTIR database should be conducted on a case-by-case basis. The general features observed in transmission spectra of heated clay minerals characterize also their ATR spectra (e.g., Villagran *et al.* 2017) (Supplementary Material).

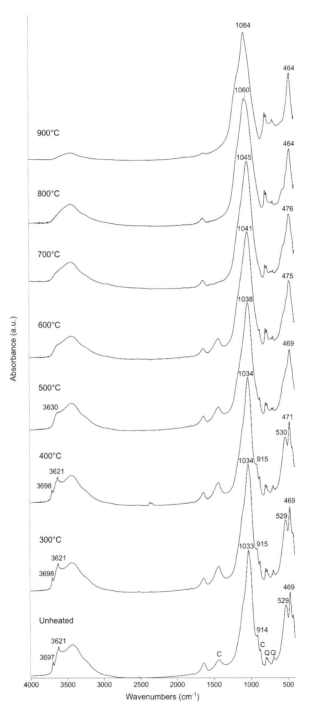

Figure 16 Spectra of phyllosilicates heated to different temperatures for four hours in an electric muffle oven, and the unheated starting material (a.u.: arbitrary units). The mixture is made of illite, kaolinite, smectite, quartz, and traces of calcite, determined by XRD (C: calcite; Q: quartz).

Particular attention should be devoted to disturbed depositional contexts (e.g., from bioturbation) and combustion features that are not physically separated from the surrounding sediment matrix (e.g., hearths, firepits), where heated and unheated clay minerals may be mixed together. Toffolo *et al.* (2017c) demonstrated that mixtures of unheated and heated clay minerals produce only some of the characteristic band shifts caused by elevated temperatures, reflecting the mixed nature of the sample (Figure 17). Ogloblin Ramírez *et al.* (2023) showed that a contribution of as little as 5 percent unheated clay minerals can produce ambiguous features in the spectra of heated clay minerals, which may lead to the underestimation of heat alteration in sediments. The authors confirmed FTIR results on loose sediments with FTIR microspectroscopy, which highlighted the occurrence of pockets of unheated clay minerals in thin sections of largely heated deposits.

3.1.2 Tectosilicates

This group includes quartz (SiO_2) and its polymorphs, feldspars, feldspathoids, and zeolites. Quartz is most common in archaeological sediments, rocks, architectural elements, ceramics, faience, and lime mortars. In its cryptocrystalline form, quartz is the main component of rocks such as flint and chalcedony, which are among the raw materials used for stone tool manufacture during prehistory. Quartz exhibits the main Si–O–Si stretching band at ~1,084 cm^{-1} with an additional Si–O band at ~1,165 cm^{-1}, a doublet at 797 and 779 cm^{-1} (Si–O stretching), shallow bands at ~695 (Si–O stretching) and ~514 cm^{-1} (Si–O bending), and a prominent band at ~460 cm^{-1} (Si–O bending) (Figure 18). In cryptocrystalline quartz, the main band may be located closer to 1,090 cm^{-1}, depending on the amount of disordered crystals, and an additional Si–O stretching band is located at 555 cm^{-1} (silanol). In moganite, which is a cryptocrystalline polymorph often mixed with the chalcedony form, the diagnostic bands are located at ~572, ~483, ~443, and ~420 cm^{-1} (Schmidt *et al.* 2013a). The crystallinity of quartz can be assessed based on the intensity of the shallow shoulder at ~1,145 cm^{-1} in the first derivative spectrum (Shoval *et al.* 1991), which is higher in well-ordered crystals, or based on the shape of the 1,084 and 695 cm^{-1} bands (Asscher *et al.* 2017). As in the case of phyllosilicates, the main Si–O–Si band of quartz appears shifted to lower wavenumbers in ATR spectra (Supplementary Material). Feldspars, feldspathoids, and zeolites occur as well in archaeological sediments, although in much smaller proportions compared to quartz. Since feldspars exhibit shallow bands at locations similar to quartz (e.g., ~646 and ~585 cm^{-1}), they are usually overlaid, and thus distinction of plagioclase from alkali feldspars in sediments is difficult with FTIR.

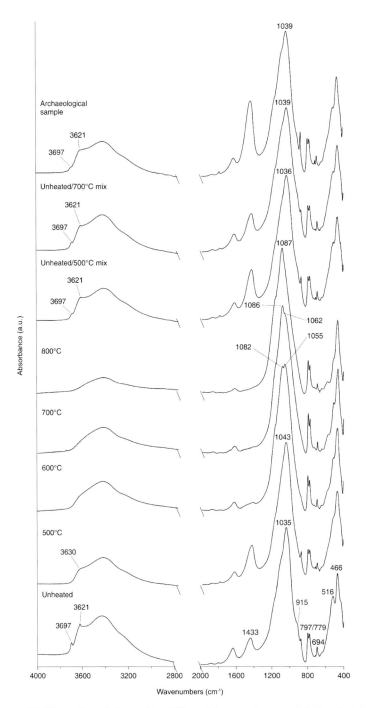

Figure 17 Clay minerals heated to different temperatures and their admixture with unheated clay minerals showing intermediate band shifts, and archaeological clay minerals for comparison from the Nesher Ramla Quarry site, Israel (a.u.: arbitrary units). Reprinted from *Journal of Archaeological Science: Reports*, 14, Toffolo *et al.* (2017c: figure 5), with permission from Elsevier.

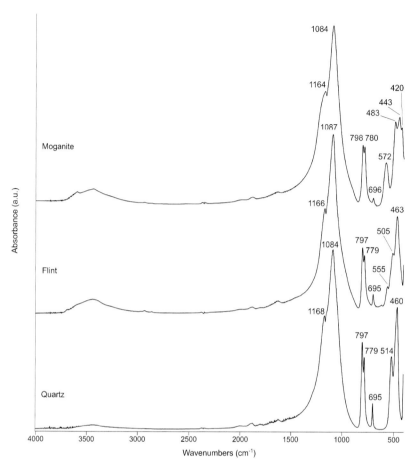

Figure 18 Transmission spectra of quartz, flint, and moganite
(a.u.: arbitrary units).

When heated to elevated temperatures, quartz may turn into its polymorphs cristobalite and tridymite, which are characterized by slightly different spectra. In cristobalite, the main band is shifted to ~1,096 cm^{-1}, the doublet is replaced by a single band at ~796 cm^{-1}, the band at ~695 cm^{-1} disappears, a new band appears at ~622 cm^{-1}, and the band at ~460 cm^{-1} shifts to ~490 cm^{-1}. In tridymite, the main band shifts to ~1,106 cm^{-1}, the doublet is replaced by a single band at ~791 cm^{-1}, the band at ~695 cm^{-1} disappears, and the band at ~460 cm^{-1} shifts to ~480 cm^{-1} (Figure 19). In archaeological settings, these changes occur when quartz is heated to temperatures above 800 °C in the presence of a flux, such as CaCO$_3$, which lowers its melting point (e.g., Toffolo *et al.* 2013b; Weiner *et al.* 2020). However, cryptocrystalline quartz may be altered by elevated temperatures alone. The ratio between the intensity

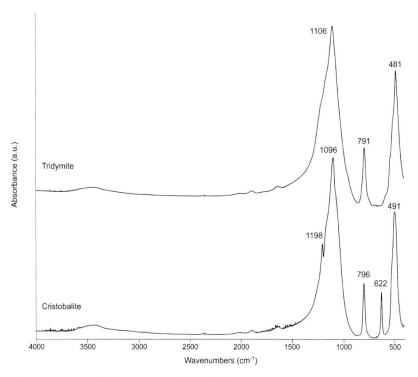

Figure 19 Transmission spectra of the high-temperature polymorphs of quartz (a.u.: arbitrary units).

of the ~514 cm^{-1} band and the intensity of the valley to its right decreases with increasing temperature, although not linearly (Weiner *et al.* 2015). In addition, the minor band at 555 cm^{-1}, which occurs mainly in flint, decreases as well (Schmidt & Frölich 2011). The main Si–O–Si band in all quartz polymorphs is located at lower wavenumbers in ATR spectra (Supplementary Material).

3.1.3 Silica

Silica is not crystalline (SiO$_2$·nH$_2$O), although it does exhibit short-range atomic order, and for that reason here it is listed under the silicates. At archaeological sites, silica occurs in its biogenic form, such as phytoliths, siliceous aggregates, and diatoms, and in its pyrogenic form, which includes obsidian, glass, and melted phytoliths. Opal, the geogenic form, is rare except in the case of stone tools. The spectrum of silica is similar to that of quartz, but with a few differences. The main band is shifted to ~1,100 cm^{-1}, the doublet is replaced by a broad band at ~800–790 cm^{-1}, and there is no band at ~695 cm^{-1}. Siliceous aggregates often contain quartz, and therefore the bands of the latter show up in

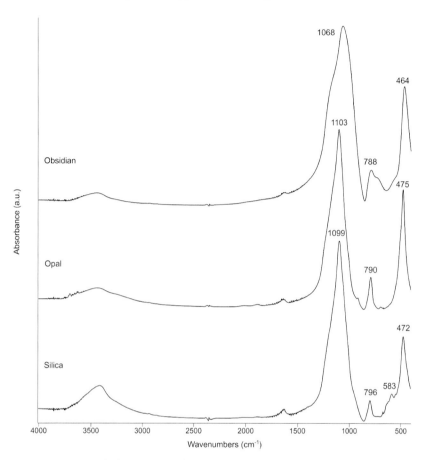

Figure 20 Transmission spectra of different types of silica (a.u.: arbitrary units).

the spectrum (Schiegl *et al.* 1994). In glass and obsidian, the main band is particularly broad and located at ~1,065 cm^{-1} (Figure 20). Like quartz, silica may turn into cristobalite and tridymite upon exposure to high temperatures (Weiner *et al.* 2020; Toffolo *et al.* 2023b). Silica, obsidian, and opal show the same shift to lower wavenumbers of the main band in ATR spectra as quartz and its polymorphs (Supplementary Material).

3.2 Carbonates

After quartz and phyllosilicates, carbonates are the third major component of archaeological sediments. Carbonates are characterized by several vibrations of the CO_3^{2-} functional group, with the major one (v_3) located in the region between 1,500 and 1,400 cm^{-1}, and shallower bands at higher and lower wavenumbers.

3.2.1 Calcite and Its Polymorphs

Calcite is the stable polymorph of $CaCO_3$ at Earth-surface conditions, and occurs in many different forms at archaeological sites. Geogenic calcite includes rocks such as limestone, chalk, travertine, cave speleothems, and marble, as well as soil formation products like calcrete. When archaeological sites lie on limestone or chalk bedrock, calcite is usually finely dispersed in sediments together with other components such as quartz and clay minerals. The same is true for eolian dust (e.g., loess) rich in calcite that may accumulate at archaeological sites. Biogenic calcite is found in the shells of some species of mollusks. Pyrogenic calcite is the main component of wood ash, lime plaster, and lime mortar. $CaCO_3$ nucleates also as the metastable polymorphs aragonite, vaterite, ikaite ($CaCO_3 \cdot 6H_2O$), monohydrocalcite ($CaCO_3 \cdot H_2O$), calcium carbonate hemihydrate ($CaCO_3 \cdot \frac{1}{2}H_2O$), and ACC. Of these, only aragonite is relevant to the analysis of archaeological sediments, since it occurs in speleothems, mollusk shells, fish otoliths, and pyrogenic products such as ash and lime plaster, whereas all other polymorphs are too unstable to preserve over long periods of time at ambient conditions (Weiner 2010; Toffolo 2021 and references therein). Monohydrocalcite, the main component of dung spherulites, may be found at recently abandoned animal enclosures, which are relevant to ethnoarchaeological studies (Shahack-Gross *et al.* 2003).

The spectrum of calcite features three main bands at ~1,420 (v_3, asymmetric stretching), ~875 (v_2, out-of-plane bending), and ~712 (v_4, in-plane bending) cm^{-1}, which are used for phase identification. Additional bands include ~2,513 ($v_1 + v_3$; shallow), ~1,798 ($v_1 + v_4$; shallow), and ~1,083 (v_1, symmetric stretching; shallow, mainly in biogenic calcite) cm^{-1}. These bands are slightly shifted in aragonite, which also includes additional bands, reflecting its different crystal structure: ~2,522 ($v_1 + v_3$; shallow), ~1,788 ($v_1 + v_4$; shallow), ~1,475 (v_3), ~1,083 (v_1), ~858 (v_2), and ~713 + 700 (v_4) cm^{-1} (Figure 21). It is interesting to note that the pyrogenic form of aragonite exhibits a shifted v_3 up to ~1,494 cm^{-1}, presumably because of its poor degree of atomic order compared to the geogenic and biogenic forms (Toffolo *et al.* 2017b: figure 2). Both polymorphs feature a shallow v_2 peak at ~845 cm^{-1} (a shoulder in aragonite), which is the vibration associated with the ^{13}C isotope (Xu *et al.* 2018). In ATR spectra, the v_3 and v_2 of calcite are located at ~1,393 and ~871 cm^{-1}, respectively. In aragonite, the same bands are located at ~1,446 and ~854 cm^{-1}, respectively (Supplementary Material).

As stated, the degree of crystallinity of calcite and aragonite is related to the formation path, and can be assessed using the grinding curve method, which allows distinguishing geogenic, biogenic, and pyrogenic forms (Regev *et al.*

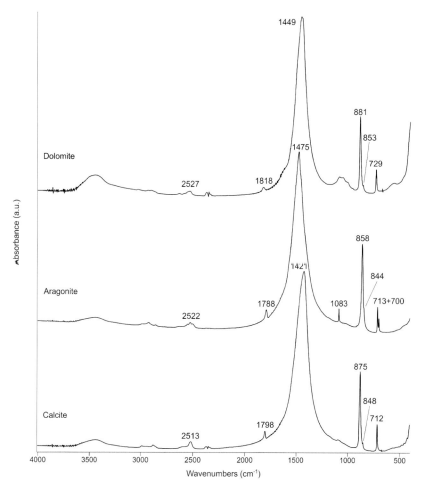

Figure 21 Transmission spectra of carbonates (a.u.: arbitrary units).

2010a; Poduska *et al.* 2011; Suzuki *et al.* 2011; Dunseth & Shahack-Gross 2018; Toffolo *et al.* 2019a) (Figure 22). In some speleothems, where structural defects caused by porosity, inclusions, crystallite size, and morphology introduce disorder in crystals, grinding curves can be complemented by XRD, which can probe specific types of structural defects, such as lattice strain and microstrain fluctuations (Xu *et al.* 2015). When calcite and aragonite are mixed, the grinding curve method cannot be applied because the two polymorphs share the v_4. Toffolo *et al.* (2019a) showed using known mixtures of calcite and aragonite that up to 20 percent content of either polymorph, the grinding curve method is not affected. For contents exceeding 20 percent, the intensity of the v_4 can be divided based on the proportions of the two polymorphs, determined by XRD in

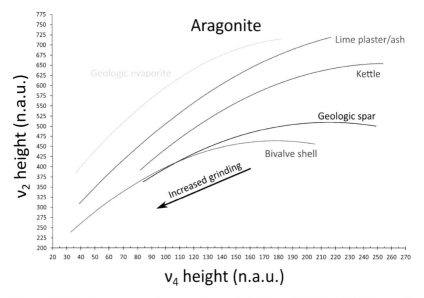

Figure 22 Grinding curves of aragonite, reprinted from Toffolo (2020: figure 2) (n.a.u.: normalized absorbance units).

archaeological samples where ratios are unknown. This is possible because calcite and aragonite exhibit similar absorptivity of the v_4 and the bands are additive (Vagenas *et al.* 2003).

The grinding curve has not been used yet in ATR mode because the intensity of the calcite bands does not behave in a consistent manner as in transmission. However, Ortiz Ruiz *et al.* (2023) recently proposed a modified version of the v_2/v_4 intensity method by Chu *et al.* (2008) for limestone and experimental and archaeological plasters analyzed using ATR. The authors demonstrated that if the v_3 falls within the FWHM range of 110–130 cm^{-1}, ATR can consistently differentiate geogenic and pyrogenic calcites based on the v_2/v_4 ratio. In addition, they found that on average the band area ratio in ATR is 1.8 ± 0.42 times higher than the v_2/v_4 intensity ratio in transmission. Similarly, Calandra *et al.* (2022) compared the normalized v_2/v_4 intensity ratio in transmission and ATR spectra by applying the ATR correction to the latter, although without monitoring the FWHM of the v_3 band. They found that the ratios are only slightly larger in ATR compared with transmission, and thus they could successfully distinguish geogenic and anthropogenic calcite. The few outliers shown in their v_2 versus v_4 intensity plots are presumably caused by lack of control over particle size.

With regard to reflection, it was demonstrated that the position and shape of the v_3 band of calcite are affected by the formation processes of the crystal.

Using FTIR microspectroscopy on micromorphology thin sections, Poduska *et al.* (2012) showed that experimental lime plaster and chalk heated to 800 °C, which are characterized by micritic calcite crystals and poor atomic order, exhibit a sharp v_3 at ~1,410 cm^{-1}. On the contrary, unheated chalk and micritic limestone exhibit a broad v_3 closer to ~1,420 cm^{-1} with an additional shoulder at ~1,470 cm^{-1}, and sparitic limestone is characterized by a broad v_3 at ~1,520 cm^{-1}. Thibodeau (2016) used the width of the v_3 at 75 percent of its intensity to identify pyrogenic calcite in micromorphology thin sections. Based on a large reference database of natural calcites and experimentally produced pyrogenic calcites, they proposed that widths smaller than 78 cm^{-1} represent pyrogenic calcite, widths between 78 and 95 cm^{-1} likely represent pyrogenic calcite, widths between 96 and 124 cm^{-1} likely represent geogenic calcite, and widths greater than 124 cm^{-1} represent geogenic calcite.

3.2.2 Dolomite

Dolomite, $CaMg(CO_3)_2$, is a carbonate mineral that contains calcium and magnesium in equal proportions. It occurs in archaeological sediments at sites located on top of dolostone bedrock or in dolostone caves, as well as inclusions in lime plaster/mortar. The presence of magnesium in the crystal structure produces a spectrum that is similar to that of calcite but with slightly shifted bands, which are located at ~2,527 ($v_1 + v_3$; shallow), ~1,818 ($v_1 + v_4$; shallow), ~1,450 (v_3), ~881 (v_2), and ~729 (v_4) cm^{-1} (Figure 21). The ^{13}C band (v_2) is located at ~853 cm^{-1}. In ATR spectra, the main bands are located at ~1,417, ~877, and ~728 cm^{-1} (Supplementary Material).

When mixed with calcite, dolomite hinders the application of the grinding curve method to assess the degree of crystallinity of calcite because the bands at 881 and 875 cm^{-1} are overlaid. As a result, the normalized intensity of the v_2 of calcite appears higher and when plotted with the normalized v_4, which instead is not affected by dolomite, the grinding curve resembles that of poorly ordered calcite even when it is geogenic. Maor *et al.* (2023) developed a calibration grinding curve using known calcite–dolomite mixtures to assess the contribution of dolomite inclusions to the grinding curve of pyrogenic calcite, and determined that a dolomite content up to 30 percent (measured by XRD in archaeological plasters) does not significantly affect the grinding curve. The v_3 bands of dolomite and calcite overlap as well, although they have similar extinction coefficients, and therefore the total band intensity does not alter the grinding curve. The authors also show that when more than 30 percent dolomite is present, it can be removed by density centrifugation in a heavy liquid.

3.3 Phosphates

Phosphates are not as abundant in sediments as silicates and carbonates, but they are major components for the interpretation of site formation processes (Weiner 2010). Phosphates occur in bones and teeth, and wherever a substantial amount of organic material degraded in the sediments. Their identification is based on the vibrations of the PO_4^{3-} functional group, mainly the v_3 located at ~1,035 cm^{-1}, which should not be mistaken with the Si–O–Si band in clay minerals (especially when the two are mixed), and the v_4 doublet between 650 and 500 cm^{-1}. Since phosphates are subject to many ion substitutions in their crystal lattice and are thus characterized by huge compositional variability, only those relevant to the study of archaeological sediments are described.

3.3.1 Calcium Phosphates

There are many types of calcium phosphate; however, the most common at archaeological sites is carbonate hydroxyapatite, $Ca_5(PO_4,CO_3)_3(OH)$, the main component of bones and teeth. This mineral features the phosphate v_3 at ~1,035 cm^{-1} (asymmetric stretching), the v_1 at ~962 cm^{-1} (symmetric stretching), and the v_4 as a doublet at ~603 and ~565 cm^{-1} (bending), with the 565 cm^{-1} peak higher than the one at 603 cm^{-1}. The carbonate vibrations are the v_3 doublet at ~1,455 and ~1,415 cm^{-1} with a shoulder at ~1,540 cm^{-1}, and the v_2 at ~872 cm^{-1}. In highly crystalline carbonate hydroxyapatite, a shallow hydroxyl band occurs at ~3,572 cm^{-1}, whereas in fluorapatite the same band is located at ~3,540 cm^{-1} (Figure 23). Carbonate hydroxyapatite can be easily distinguished from its geogenic counterpart, which does not contain carbonates and it is seldom found in archaeological sediments. In addition, geogenic hydroxyapatite and synthetic carbonate hydroxyapatite exhibit a peak at ~575 cm^{-1} instead of 565 cm^{-1} in the doublet of the phosphate v_4 (Figure 23). When fluoride (F$^-$) is present in groundwater, it is usually incorporated in bone mineral, which transforms into fluoridated carbonate hydroxyapatite, $Ca_5(PO_4,CO_3)_3(OH,F)$. This phase is characterized by the same spectrum as the non-fluoridated form, except for the v_4 doublet, where the height of the 603 cm^{-1} peak exceeds the height of the 565 cm^{-1} peak (Geiger & Weiner 1993). However, this is not the case in ATR spectra (Aufort *et al.* 2016), which therefore cannot be used to identify the fluoridated form (Supplementary Material). As in the previous case, the geogenic counterpart does not contain carbonate groups (Figure 23). Fluoride substitutes for hydroxyl (OH$^-$) groups in more symmetrical locations within the crystal lattice, and substitutions progress over time until no hydroxyl is left and the mineral is called carbonate fluorapatite, $Ca_5(PO_4,CO_3)_3F$. For that reason, the fluoridated form is more resistant to

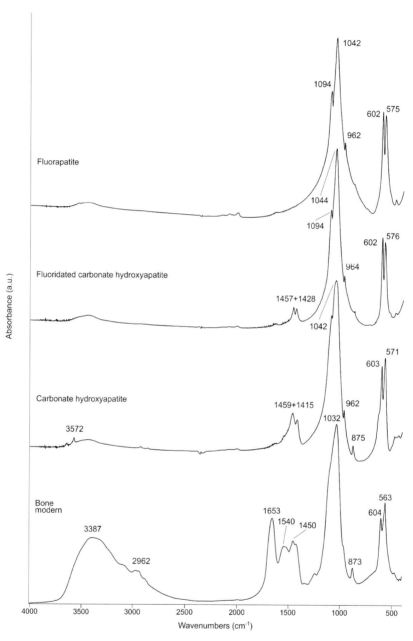

Figure 23 Transmission spectra of calcium phosphates (a.u.: arbitrary units).

chemical weathering (Newesely 1989; LeGeros 1991). In fact, fossil bone of very old age is invariably composed of fluoridated carbonate hydroxyapatite or fluorapatite (e.g., Piga *et al.* 2011). The ATR spectra of all calcium phosphates exhibit bands slightly shifted toward lower wavenumbers, which often show lower or higher intensity compared to transmission spectra (Supplementary Material).

As described, the ratios of type A (1,540 cm^{-1}) and type B (1,415 cm^{-1}) carbonates to phosphate bands can inform on carbonate content, and therefore on the degree of diagenesis (Wright & Schwarcz 1996; Sponheimer & Lee-Thorp 1999). Calcite may form in bones as a secondary phase, and its propor-tion can be assessed by dividing the intensity of the calcite v_4 at ~712 cm^{-1} by the intensity of the phosphate v_3 at ~1,035 cm^{-1} (Dal Sasso *et al.* 2016). Collagen content may be estimated by dividing the intensity of the amide I band at ~1,650 cm^{-1} by the intensity of the phosphate v_3 (Trueman *et al.* 2004) (Table 2).

Another means of assessing the degree of diagenesis of carbonate hydroxy-apatite is to determine its crystallinity by calculating the IRSF. Values up to 3 are typical of modern bone, whereas fossil bone produces higher values up to 7 for extremely altered specimens (Weiner & Bar-Yosef 1990). Modern enamel values fall around 3.8, with heavily weathered specimens reaching close to 5

Table 2 Band intensity ratios of biogenic carbonate hydroxyapatite.

Parameter	Ratio	Reference
Carbonate content	1,415 cm^{-1}/1,035 cm^{-1}	Wright and Schwarcz (1996)
Carbonate content	1,540 cm^{-1}/603 cm^{-1}; 1,415 cm^{-1}/603 cm^{-1}	Featherstone *et al.* (1984); Sponheimer and Lee-Thorp (1999)
Relative carbonate content	1,415 cm^{-1}/1,540 cm^{-1}	Sponheimer and Lee-Thorp (1999)
Calcite content	712 cm^{-1}/1,035 cm^{-1}	Dal Sasso *et al.* (2016)
Collagen content with respect to phosphates	1,650 cm^{-1}/1,035 cm^{-1}	Trueman *et al.* (2004)
Collagen content with respect to carbonates	1,650 cm^{-1}/1,415 cm^{-1}	Thompson *et al.* (2013)
IRSF	(603 cm^{-1} + 567 cm^{-1})/595 cm^{-1}	Termine and Posner (1966); Weiner and Bar-Yosef (1990)
Crystallinity	1,060 cm^{-1}/1,075 cm^{-1}	Lebon *et al.* (2010)
Crystallinity (upon heating)	630 cm^{-1}/603 cm^{-1}	Thompson *et al.* (2013)

(Asscher *et al.* 2011b; Richard *et al.* 2022). The IRSF should not be used to compare carbonate hydroxyapatite with its fluoridated form, as they are two different phases that produce different peak intensities (Weiner 2010). The phosphate v_3 may also provide information on crystallinity. Lebon *et al.* (2010) showed that the ratio of the intensity of the v_3 at 1,060 and 1,075 cm^{-1} in bones increases with diagenesis (and exposure to elevated temperatures), and this value is consistent with the IRSF of the same bones (Table 2). Beasley *et al.* (2014) demonstrated that transmission and ATR produce comparable IRSF values and carbonate-to-phosphate ratios, whereas DRIFT cannot distinguish between modern and fossil bones. Therefore, it is advisable to use the same acquisition mode to analyze a given set of samples.

As explained, the IRSF does not distinguish the opposing effects of particle size and atomic order in carbonate hydroxyapatite crystals. Asscher *et al.* (2011b) used the grinding curve method to monitor the particle size effect, which is represented by the FWHM of the ~1,035 cm^{-1} band (Figure 24). This value is plotted against the IRSF to produce trendlines typical of carbonate hydroxyapatite at different states of preservation. Increased grinding reduces

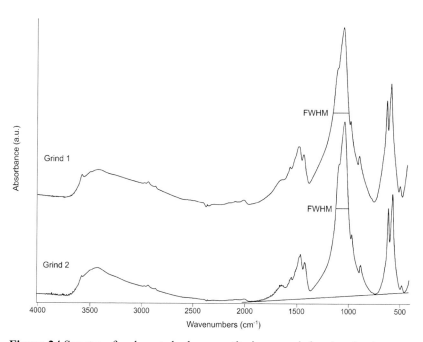

Figure 24 Spectra of carbonate hydroxyapatite in enamel showing the decrease in FWHM values upon repeated grinding, and the baseline used for the calculation of band intensity (a.u.: arbitrary units).

particle size and increases the IRSF, whereas the offset between trendlines reflects different degrees of atomic order, with higher offset compared to a fresh standard indicative of greater diagenesis (Asscher *et al.* 2011a). This method can be applied to bone mineral, dentine, cementum, and enamel, provided that comparisons between fossil and fresh material are made based on the same species or a close relative, since not all species mineralize crystals with the same initial degree of atomic order (Asscher *et al.* 2011b; Richard *et al.* 2022; Toffolo & Richard 2024) (Figure 25). Dal Sasso *et al.* (2018) proposed to improve the grinding curve method by replacing the FWHM of the phosphate v_3 with the FW at 85 percent of the intensity of the 603 cm^{-1} peak in the v_4 doublet, as the latter is the result of only one vibration and thus offers a more reliable reference for the crystallinity of carbonate hydroxyapatite, as opposed to the v_3, which is produced from the contribution of different vibrations.

Exposure to elevated temperatures increases the crystallinity of bone carbonate hydroxyapatite, and thus the IRSF (Weiner & Bar-Yosef 1990; Stiner *et al.* 1995) up to 900 °C, when it starts decreasing due to melting and sintering of hydroxyapatite crystals (Mamede *et al.* 2018). Under 500 °C, bones lose water, as reflected by the disappearance of the broad band at 3,600–2,600 cm^{-1} (van

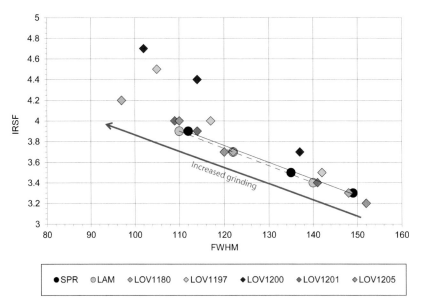

Figure 25 Grinding curves of modern springbok (*Antidorcas marsupialis*) and lamb (*Ovis aries*) enamel and fossil antelope enamel, reprinted from *Quaternary Geochronology*, 69, Richard *et al.* (2022: figure 4), with permission from Elsevier.

Hoesel *et al.* 2019). In addition, the amide I (~1,650 cm^{-1}) and amide II (~1,548 cm^{-1}) bands lose intensity until they disappear. This can be monitored using the ratio between amide I and phosphate v_3 bands. At temperatures above 500 °C, the OH$^-$ libration band representing the intake of hydroxyl appears at ~630 cm^{-1} and acquires intensity with increasing temperature (Shaw 2022). This process is quantified by calculating the ratio between this band and the phosphate v_4 peak at ~603 cm^{-1} (Thompson *et al.* 2013). The spectrum of calcined bones exhibits the phosphate v_3 shifted to higher wavenumbers and additional bands at ~3,572, ~1,090, and ~630 cm^{-1}, although the first two are also found in extensively weathered bones (Weiner 2010). Reidsma *et al.* (2016) showed that the ~630 cm^{-1} band does not appear in bones heated to 700 °C under reducing conditions, and therefore it is insufficient as a proxy for heat alteration. Shaw (2022) demonstrated that the same band appears only above 537 °C in bones burned in non-reducing conditions. In addition, extensively fluoridated bones are not likely to develop this band at high temperatures, since part of the hydroxyl groups have been replaced by fluoride. The intensity of this band is also affected by post-depositional chemical alteration of heated bones, for instance at low pH (Reidsma 2022). Gallo *et al.* (2023) showed that heating duration also plays a role in the appearance of these additional bands. For instance, the ~1,090 and ~630 cm^{-1} bands appear as shoulders in the spectra of bones after nine hours of heating at 550 °C, whereas after ten minutes of heating, the same bands appear at 750 °C. The IRSF is similarly affected, with bones heated to 550 °C for forty-eight hours exhibiting IRSF values typical of bones heated to higher temperatures for shorter periods of time. Bones heated to 750 °C for forty-eight hours show a decrease of the IRSF typical of bones heated to temperatures above 900 °C.

3.3.2 Authigenic Phosphates

Authigenic phosphates are minerals that form in the archaeological record after sediment deposition, especially in places where large amounts of organic material are embedded in sediments, such as animal enclosures, storage facilities, garbage dumps, and guano accumulations in caves. When organic matter decays, it releases phosphate ions and acids, which lower the pH of sediments. Acidic groundwater favors the dissolution of the more soluble minerals, such as biogenic aragonite and pyrogenic calcite, which release calcium ions. The latter react with phosphate to form authigenic phosphates. The type of phosphate mineral is determined by the nature of the ions and the pH of sediments; however, the first mineral to form is often carbonate hydroxyapatite, which exhibits the same spectrum as its biogenic counterpart in bones. When the pH drops under 7, crandallite forms at low phosphate concentrations, whereas montgomeryite forms at high phosphate concentrations. Further drops in pH over time cause the nucleation of less and less soluble phosphate minerals, with the more common in cave settings being variscite, leucophosphite, and taranakite (Karkanas *et al.* 2000). Other rare authigenic phosphate minerals that may be encountered in archaeological sediments are brushite, whitlockite, richellite, jahnsite, wavellite, vivianite, bobierrite, and purpurite (Table 3) (Chukanov 2014). Each of these nucleates under specific chemical environments, and therefore may inform on past water regimes and post-depositional processes (Weiner 2010).

Authigenic phosphates are characterized by poor atomic order, and seldom resemble their geogenic counterparts. This makes them of difficult identification when they occur in sediments, mixed with clay minerals, quartz, or silica. A rule of thumb is that authigenic phosphates in archaeological sediments tend to exhibit band locations similar to the geogenic phosphates, although much broader, which reflects their poor atomic order (Weiner 2010). In general, authigenic phosphates exhibit a broad band between $4{,}000\text{--}3{,}000$ cm^{-1} related to the hydroxyl groups, on which shallower peaks and shoulders may help

Table 3 Authigenic phosphate minerals and their chemical formula

Authigenic phosphate mineral	Chemical formula
Carbonate hydroxyapatite	$Ca_5(PO_4,CO_3)_3(OH)$
Crandallite	$CaAl_3(PO_4)_2(OH)_5 \cdot (H_2O)$
Montgomeryite	$Ca_4MgAl_4(PO_4)_6(OH)_4 \cdot 12H_2O$
Variscite	$AlPO_4 \cdot 2H_2O$
Leucophosphite	$KFe^{3+}_2(PO_4)_2(OH) \cdot 2H_2O$
Taranakite	$(K,Na)_3(Al,Fe^{3+})_5(PO_4)_2(HPO_4)_6 \cdot 18H_2O$
Brushite	$CaHPO_4 \cdot 2H_2O$
Whitlockite	$Ca_9(Mg,Fe^{2+})(PO_4)_6(PO_3OH)$
Richellite	$CaFe^{3+}_2(PO_4)_2(OH,F)_2$
Jahnsite[a]	$XM1M2_2M3_2(H_2O)_8(OH)_2(PO_4)_4$
Wavellite	$Al_3(PO_4)_2(OH,F)_3 \cdot 5H_2O$
Vivianite	$Fe^{2+}_3(PO_4)_2 \cdot 8H_2O$
Bobierrite	$Mg_3(PO_4)_2 \cdot 8H_2O$
Purpurite	$Mn^{3+}PO_4$

Note that slight variations in composition are possible since phosphates are prone to ion substitutions; these translate into changes in the infrared spectrum. [a]: the jahnsite group is characterized by high cation variability (Fe, Mg, Mn, Al, Na, and Ca), although Fe^{3+} is usually dominant at the M3 site.

distinguish specific minerals. All authigenic phosphates include at least one band between ~1,200–900 cm^{-1}, which may feature multiple peaks, and several shallow bands under 900 cm^{-1} (Figures 26–29). The ATR spectra of authigenic phosphates exhibit bands slightly shifted toward lower wavenumbers, which often show lower or higher intensity compared to transmission spectra (Supplementary Material).

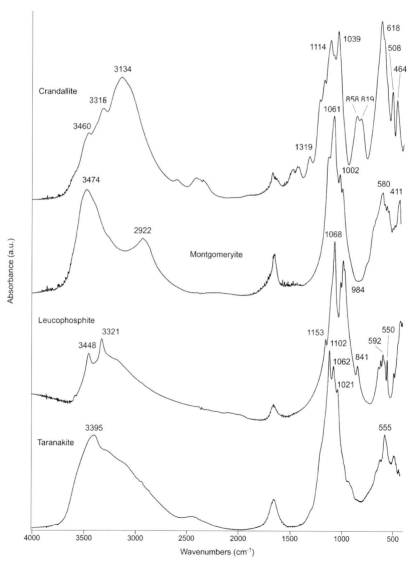

Figure 26 Transmission spectra of authigenic phosphates (a.u.: arbitrary units).

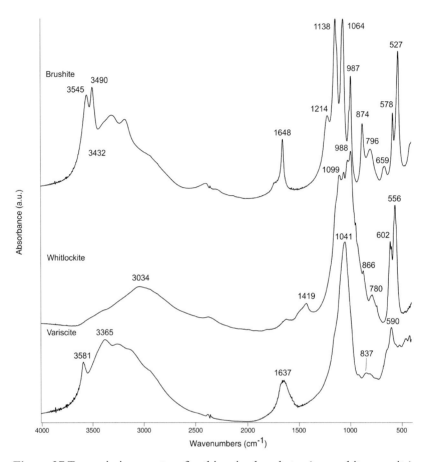

Figure 27 Transmission spectra of authigenic phosphates (a.u.: arbitrary units).

3.4 Oxides and Hydroxides

The most common oxides and hydroxides found in archaeological sediments are iron compounds, namely hematite, goethite, and limonite, which are the main components of materials of archaeological importance such as red and yellow ochre pigments (e.g., Domingo *et al.* 2012). All these minerals are characterized by a sloping spectrum due to their opacity. Hematite, Fe_2O_3, exhibits two prominent bands at ~550 and ~470 cm^{-1}; goethite, $FeO(OH)$, exhibits three diagnostic bands at ~900, ~800, and ~600 cm^{-1}; limonite, $FeO(OH) \cdot nH_2O$, includes bands at ~1,030, ~900, and ~800 cm^{-1} (Figure 30). The position of these bands may change by a few wavenumbers, depending on the composition of the original ore, which can vary considerably. In fact, these minerals are often found mixed with clay minerals, calcite, and quartz, to the point that the diagnostic bands may be of

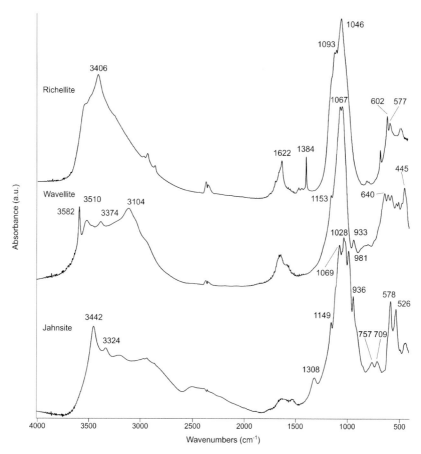

Figure 28 Transmission spectra of authigenic phosphates (a.u.: arbitrary units). Jahnsite is of the CaMnMg type. The sharp band at 1,384 cm^{-1} represents nitrates.

difficult identification. In ATR, the position of hematite bands is shifted toward lower wavenumbers, as well as the 900 and 600 cm^{-1} bands in goethite and the 900 cm^{-1} band in limonite (Supplementary Material).

3.5 Less Common Salts

Some types of salts, including nitrates, sulfates, and oxalates, are rather rare in the archaeological record, but may be useful indicators of recent and past water chemistry or site occupation.

3.5.1 Nitrates

Nitrates are salts that usually form on or close to exposed sediment surfaces, such as standing sections, due to capillary action upon drying (Weiner 2010).

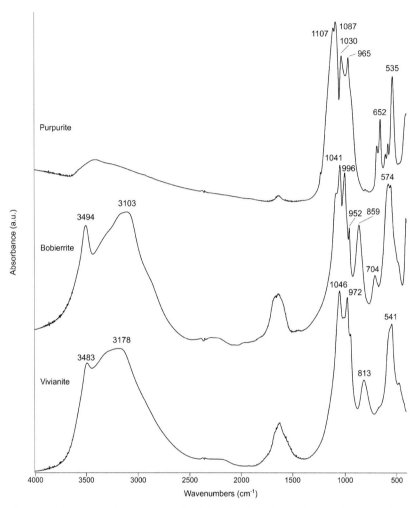

Figure 29 Transmission spectra of authigenic phosphates (a.u.: arbitrary units). Note that vivianite and bobierrite, which are characterized by similar crystal structure (Table 3), exhibit similar spectra.

Therefore, they are not representative of site formation processes, and being highly soluble, they cannot be uniquely linked to post-depositional processes that took place in the distant past. However, they may be observed in sediments. Sodium nitrate ($NaNO_3$) and potassium nitrate (KNO_3) both exhibit a prominent band at 1,384 cm^{-1}, and are distinguished based on the occurrence of a shallower band at 836 (sodium) or 825 (potassium) cm^{-1} (Figure 31). The ATR spectra of both nitrates exhibit bands slightly shifted toward lower wavenumbers (Supplementary Material).

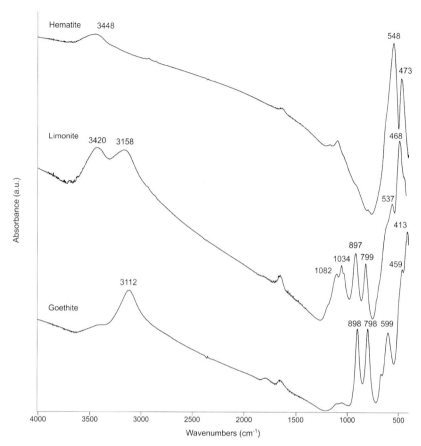

Figure 30 Transmission spectra of iron oxides and hydroxides (a.u.: arbitrary units). Note the sloping baseline caused by the opaque nature of the sample. The bands at 1,082 and 1,034 cm^{-1} in limonite are due to quartz and clay minerals, respectively.

3.5.2 Sulfates

Like nitrates, sulfates form upon water evaporation in sediments. Gypsum ($CaSO_4 \cdot 2H_2O$) is the most common form, often found as secondary needle-shaped crystals or aggregates in sediments (e.g., Birkenfeld *et al.* 2020). Gypsum can also be used as raw material for plaster production (e.g., Akyuz *et al.* 2015). Upon heating up to 400 °C, gypsum is left with half water molecule and thus turns into plaster of Paris, or bassanite ($CaSO_4 \cdot \frac{1}{2}H_2O$), which can be rehydrated to form a moldable putty. At higher temperatures, anhydrite ($CaSO_4$) forms, which cannot be rehydrated (except for rare cases in which anhydrite is preserved in the presence of water: e.g., Tang *et al.* 2019). Anhydrite may be

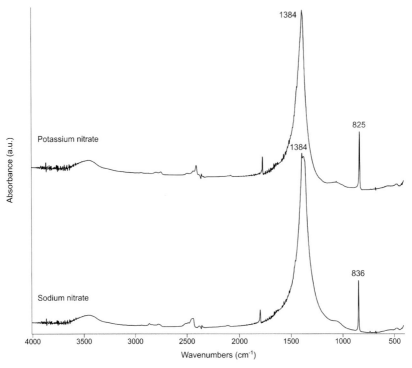

Figure 31 Transmission spectra of nitrates (a.u.: arbitrary units).

found in ash produced from tamarisk wood, which is a species that mineralizes bassanite (Weiner *et al.* 2021). The spectrum of gypsum features several broad bands in the 3,600–3,000 cm^{-1} region, shallow bands at ~1,685 and ~1,621 cm^{-1}, a prominent doublet at ~1,141–1,116 cm^{-1}, and shallower bands at ~670 and ~602 cm^{-1}. In bassanite, there are shallow bands at ~3,612, ~3,558, ~1,621, ~675, ~661, ~614, and ~596 cm^{-1}, and the prominent doublet becomes a single peak at ~1,153 cm^{-1} with a shoulder at ~1,115 cm^{-1}. Anhydrite exhibits only the band at ~1,153 cm^{-1} and a set of sharp bands at ~676, ~614, and ~595 cm^{-1} (Figure 32). Potassium, magnesium, and barium sulfates are salts usually found in salt pans and evaporites. Potassium sulfate (K_2SO_4) exhibits sharp bands at ~1,114 and ~617 cm^{-1}; magnesium sulfate heptahydrate, or epsomite ($MgSO_4 \cdot 7H_2O$), features a broad band between 4,000 and 2,700 cm^{-1}, and at ~1,663, ~1,091, and ~616 cm^{-1}; barium sulfate, or barite ($BaSO_4$), is characterized by a triplet at ~1,180, ~1,118, and ~1,084 cm^{-1}, a shallow band at ~982 cm^{-1}, and a doublet at ~635 and ~610 cm^{-1} (Figure 33). The ATR spectra of sulfates exhibit bands slightly shifted toward lower wavenumbers (Supplementary Material).

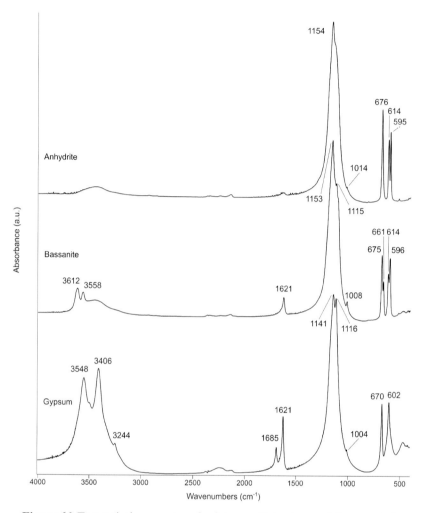

Figure 32 Transmission spectra of calcium sulfates (a.u.: arbitrary units).

3.5.3 Oxalates

Oxalates are salts produced by many plants; however, only calcium oxalates may be encountered in archaeological settings, and under very specific conditions because they are quickly degraded by bacteria once they are deposited in sediments. Whewellite ($CaC_2O_4 \cdot H_2O$) and weddellite ($CaC_2O_4 \cdot 2H_2O$) may be preserved in recently abandoned animal enclosures, either as a component of dung or fodder (Shahack-Gross *et al.* 2004b). Whewellite is characterized by broad bands between 3,700 and 2,800 cm^{-1}, prominent bands at ~1,622 and ~1,317 cm^{-1}, and a series of shallower bands under 1,000 cm^{-1}. The spectrum of weddellite is similar, although only one broad band occurs at ~3,445 cm^{-1}, the

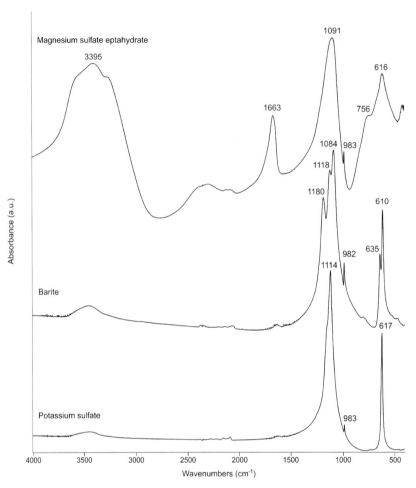

Figure 33 Transmission spectra of sulfates (a.u.: arbitrary units).

prominent bands are shifted to ~1,647 and ~1,324 cm^{-1}, and the shallow bands under 1,000 cm^{-1} are broader and in slightly different positions (Figure 34). The ATR spectra of both oxalates exhibit bands slightly shifted toward lower wavenumbers (Supplementary Material).

3.6 Organics

Organic materials at archaeological sites are usually preserved only under favorable conditions, such as absence of water (e.g., desert environment) and absence of oxygen (e.g., waterlogged sediments), unless they are located in a "protected niche" such as collagen in bone, or underwent some kind of transformation through human agency such as burning, which can preserve plant material in

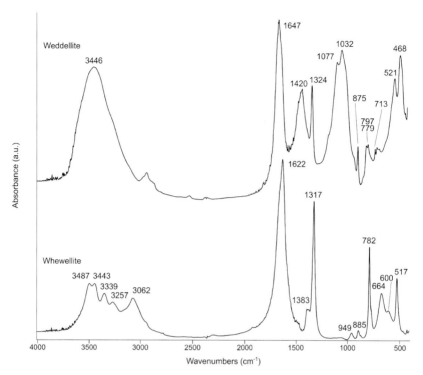

Figure 34 Transmission spectra of calcium oxalates (a.u.: arbitrary units). In weddellite, the bands at 1,420, 875, and 713 cm^{-1} belong to calcite, the bands at 1,077, 797, and 779 cm^{-1} belong to quartz, and the bands at 1,032, 521, and 468 cm^{-1} belong to clay minerals.

charred form. Organics of archaeological relevance include proteins, polysaccharides, humic acids, resins, and waxes. In the following spectra, prominent bands repeatedly occur in the 3,000–2,800 cm^{-1} region: ~2,950 cm^{-1} (CH$_3$ vibrations), ~2,920 cm^{-1} (CH$_2$ vibrations), ~2,870 cm^{-1} (CH$_3$ vibrations), and ~2,850 cm^{-1} (CH$_2$ vibrations). Other bands are common throughout the samples in the region between 1,800 and 1,000 cm^{-1}: ~1,700 cm^{-1} (C=O), ~1,620 cm^{-1} (C=C), ~1,460 cm^{-1} (CH$_3$ and CH$_2$), and ~1,200–1,000 cm^{-1} (C–O in cellulose) (van der Marel & Beutelspacher 1976; Lin-Vien *et al.* 1991).

Collagen is the main protein in the connective tissue of mammals, and as such it is the most important organic molecule found at archaeological sites, given its suitability for radiocarbon dating, carbon and nitrogen stable isotopes analysis, and species fingerprinting. The spectrum of collagen exhibits a broad OH$^-$ band at ~3,412 cm^{-1}, the amide I band at ~1,650 cm^{-1}, the amide II band at ~1,540 cm^{-1}, the proline band at ~1,450 cm^{-1}, and the amide III band at

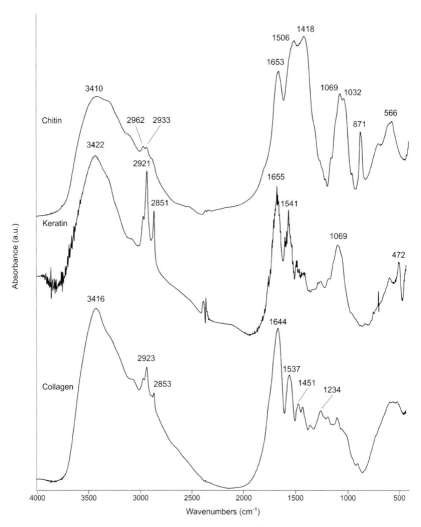

Figure 35 Transmission spectra of bone collagen, keratin, and chitin (a.u.: arbitrary units).

~1,235 cm^{-1} (Figure 35). In diagenetically altered bone, where collagen is degraded, only the more prominent amide I band may be visible (DeNiro & Weiner 1988; Yizhaq *et al.* 2005). Keratin, a protein that is the main component of hair, wool, nails, claws, hooves, feathers, horns, and the outer layer of skin in some vertebrates, is characterized by a spectrum similar to that of collagen (e.g., Bertrand *et al.* 2014). Other organic molecules that may be encountered at archaeological sites under exceptional circumstances are chitin, a polysaccharide produced by many arthropods that exhibits several bands below 1,700 cm^{-1}

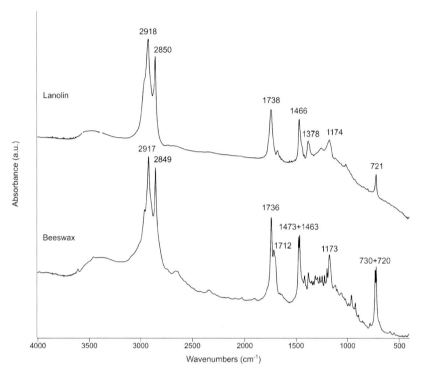

Figure 36 Transmission spectra of beeswax and lanolin (a.u.: arbitrary units). Note the sloping baseline caused by poor pressing of the pellet, due to the sticky nature of the sample.

(e.g., Friesem *et al.* 2021b); beeswax, a wax composed of fatty acids and alcohols produced by honey bees, including a major doublet at ~2,917 and ~2,849 cm^{-1} and several shallower bands below 1,800 cm^{-1} (e.g., Regert *et al.* 2001); and lanolin, a wax that comprises long-chain waxy esters produced by wool-bearing animals, with a spectrum similar to that of beeswax although with less bands below 1,800 cm^{-1} (e.g., Bergamonti *et al.* 2022) (Figure 36). Band positions in ATR spectra do not show significant differences compared with transmission (Supplementary Material).

Materials of plant origin include cellulose and wood, and their charred forms. Cellulose is characterized by a broad OH^{-} band at ~3,400 cm^{-1} and prominent polysaccharide bands between 1,500 and 800 cm^{-1}. Wood, on the other hand, exhibits shallower bands in the latter region. Fresh charcoal exhibits shallow and broad bands at ~3,430 (O–H) and ~1,560 (C=C aromatic stretching) cm^{-1}. Fossil charcoal exhibits a prominent, broad OH^{-} band at ~3,380 cm^{-1}, and sharper carboxylate bands at ~1,570 and ~1,380 cm^{-1}. Upon diagenesis, additional bands of carboxylic acid appear at ~1,700 and

~1,260 cm^{-1} (Cohen-Ofri *et al.* 2006; Rebollo *et al.* 2008). Humic acids are commonly found in waterlogged sediments rich in partially decayed plant material, such as peat (e.g., Toffolo *et al.* 2017a), and exhibit a broad band at ~3,370 cm^{-1} and prominent bands of aromatic moieties between 1,800 and 1,000 cm^{-1} (Figure 37).

Among the resins, amber and copal may be encountered at archaeological sites in the form of artifacts (e.g., Guiliano *et al.* 2007; Zhao *et al.* 2023). Both resins exhibit a broad doublet at ~2,930–2,868 cm^{-1}, and several terpene bands below 1,800 cm^{-1}: ~1,380 cm^{-1} corresponds to CH$_3$ vibrations, ~1,200–1,000 cm^{-1} are caused by (CH$_3$)$_2$CH– vibrations, and the prominent band at ~888 cm^{-1} is the result of CH vibrations. Birch and pine tar were used in prehistoric times as binder in composite tools, for instance to haft spear points. They are sometimes found as residues on stone artifacts (e.g., Schmidt *et al.* 2023). Pine tar exhibits prominent bands at ~2,928 and ~2,852 cm^{-1}, and many shallower bands under 1,800 cm^{-1} (Figure 38). Similar bands occur in bitumen, also known as asphalt, a constituent of petroleum, with the difference that the prominent band at 1,710 cm^{-1} and smaller bands under 1,300 cm^{-1} are absent (e.g., Burger *et al.* 2016). Synthetic resins derived from fossil hydrocarbons, such as epoxy and polyester, are not found at archaeological sites; however, they may represent a contaminant in some archaeological materials that undergo consolidation for curation purposes, and they are present in petrographic and micromorphology thin sections analyzed with FTIR microspectroscopy. Both compounds exhibit a broad OH$^-$ band at ~3,100–2,850 cm^{-1}, and several bands below 1,800 cm^{-1}. Polyester can be distinguished from epoxy based on three prominent bands at ~1,735 (C=O), ~744, and ~701 cm^{-1} (C–H), whereas epoxy exhibits bands at ~1,509 (C=C) and ~828 cm^{-1} (C–H) that are absent in polyester (Figure 39).

Among the waxes, another compound produced from fossil hydrocarbons is paraffin, which is a common preservative for archaeological materials, especially bones. Paraffin exhibits a few sharp, diagnostic bands at ~2,957, ~2,918, ~2,850, ~1,466, ~1,378, ~889, and ~720 cm^{-1} (Figure 40). Carnauba wax, derived from the leaves of *Copernicia prunifera*, may be found at archaeological sites in South America, where leaves were used to manufacture ropes, bags, and fabric, and the wax was used as mastic (e.g., Cristiani *et al.* 2008). Carnauba exhibits an infrared spectrum similar to that of beeswax; however, it can be distinguished from the latter based on the occurrence of a triplet at ~1,632, ~1,606, and ~1,588 cm^{-1}, and a sharp band at ~1,515 cm^{-1} (Figure 40). Band positions in ATR spectra of organic compounds do not show significant differences compared with transmission (Supplementary Material).

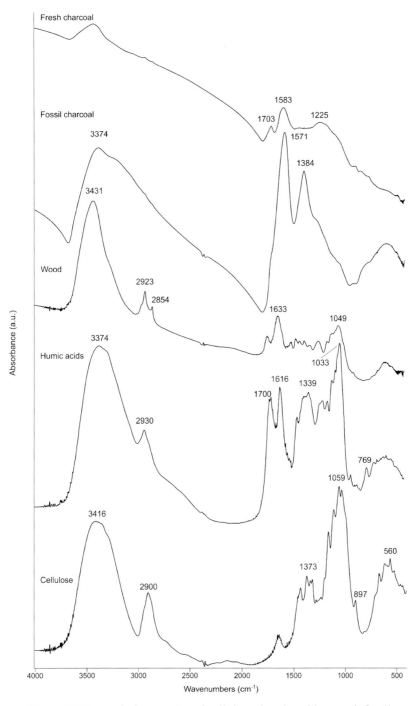

Figure 37 Transmission spectra of cellulose, humic acids, wood, fossil charcoal, and fresh charcoal (a.u.: arbitrary units). Note the sloping baseline in charcoal, caused by the opaque nature of the sample.

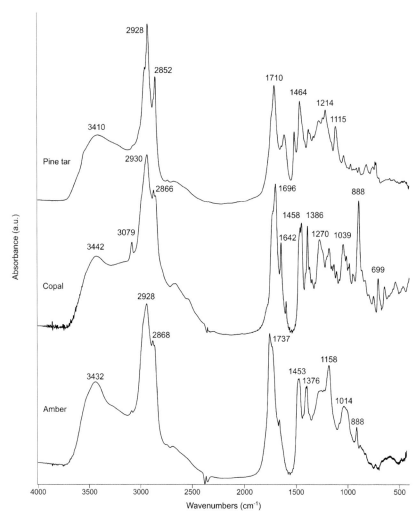

Figure 38 Transmission spectra of amber, copal, and pine tar
(a.u.: arbitrary units).

4 Applications to Archaeological Sediments and Their Contents

4.1 Preservation of the Archaeological Record

The occurrence of certain phases in the archaeological record has been shown to be indicative of chemical processes that affect sedimentary deposits and the materials embedded in them, thus facilitating the assessment of the integrity of archaeological contexts (Weiner 2010). Fourier transform infrared spectroscopy is particularly effective in identifying minerals and poorly crystalline phases produced in different chemical environments, which can be linked to specific

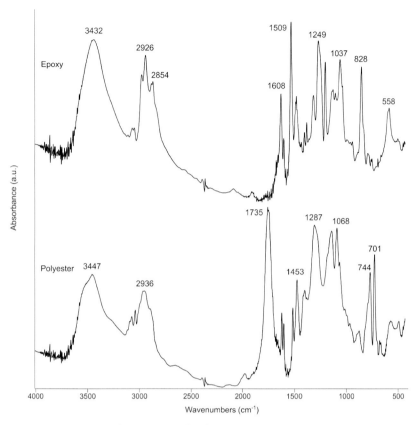

Figure 39 Transmission spectra of polyester and epoxy (a.u.: arbitrary units).

post-depositional processes, such as bone dissolution. In addition, the same processes alter the isotopic composition and crystallinity of geogenic, biogenic, and pyrogenic materials, which record environmental and chronological information used to reconstruct site occupation; probing their state of preservation using FTIR provides a measure of how accurate is the information that can be obtained.

4.1.1 Post-Depositional Processes at Archaeological Sites

Post-depositional processes alter layers of sediments and their contents after deposition, and are referred to as diagenesis. Diagenetic processes include both mechanical and chemical alteration of archaeological sediments and materials, and are active in open-air contexts and sheltered sites (i.e., caves and rock shelters). Mechanical alteration is prevalent at open-air sites, which are usually located in active sedimentary systems subject to deposition, erosion, and

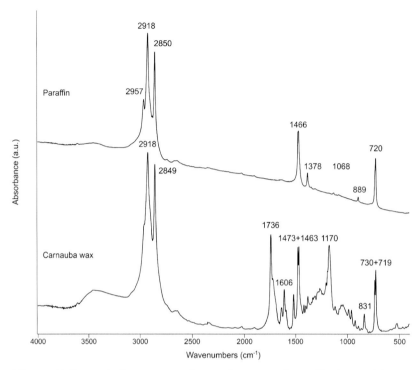

Figure 40 Transmission spectra of carnauba wax and paraffin (a.u.: arbitrary units). Note the sloping baseline caused by poor pressing of the pellet, due to the sticky nature of the sample.

deflation. Chemical alteration, including compaction, cryoturbation, dissolution, and reprecipitation, is found at both open-air and sheltered sites. Pedogenesis, which may be placed in the chemical alteration category, occurs only in open contexts. Dissolution and reprecipitation processes of minerals are usually not visible to the naked eye but can be easily detected using FTIR spectroscopy, and are especially important in caves and rock shelters. In addition, the combination of FTIR with micromorphology thin sections provides the necessary spatial dimension to phase identification (e.g., Goldberg & Berna 2010; Mentzer 2014).

The key to understand these processes is to know under which environmental setting a given mineral is thermodynamically stable. The main factors governing this setting are groundwater chemistry and flow, which favor alteration. When water enriched with different ions passes through sediments, it reacts with the latter and changes its chemistry until it attains a state of equilibrium. If this water is not replaced, chemical reactions cannot proceed. However, if water is replaced by new water due to gravity flow or other means, such as capillary action caused by evaporation, chemical reactions are resumed until equilibrium is achieved, thus leading to further chemical alteration of the sediment. Therefore, the rate of the reactions depends on the rate of the water flow. For this reason, open-air sites exposed to rainwater are the most prone to chemical alteration, which is enhanced in porous sedimentary contexts (gravel and sand). Temperature affects the process as well, with higher temperatures increasing the rate of alteration. Since archaeological sediments and materials mainly consist of minerals, their stability depends on how they react when exposed to water characterized by a particular chemistry (Karkanas & Goldberg 2019).

As we have seen, the most common minerals encountered in the archaeological record are silicates, carbonates, and phosphates. Silicates such as quartz and feldspars are very stable under a wide range of pH values, whereas carbonates and phosphates are more chemically reactive. Calcite is stable when the pH of groundwater is above 8. However, the pH drops below 8 when groundwater is rich in carbonic acid. This component forms when rainwater dissolves atmospheric CO_2, and when surface waters react with organic matter in sediments, which releases CO_2 upon oxidation. When this slightly acidic water migrates down sediment profiles, it dissolves calcite until it gets saturated, unless it is constantly replaced by acidic water, in which case calcite eventually dissolves completely. In places where a large amount of calcite is present in sediments (e.g., on limestone bedrock or within ash layers), this can act as a buffer and slow down the dissolution process. If water is not replaced, it may evaporate by capillarity and thus lead to the precipitation of secondary calcite. Due to Ostwald ripening, secondary crystals are larger and more ordered at the atomic level compared to the parent material. For instance, the dissolution of micritic calcite in limestone tends to produce sparitic calcite. In wood ash, pyrogenic calcite is poorly ordered and thus produces more ordered crystals upon dissolution and reprecipitation, more similar to geogenic calcite. This process can be monitored using the grinding curve method, and in thin section using FTIR microspectroscopy in reflection mode (Regev *et al.* 2010a, 2011; Poduska *et al.* 2012; Thibodeau 2016).

Since aragonite is more soluble than calcite and carbonate hydroxyapatite, it is supposed to be the first mineral to dissolve. Therefore, if the shells of species that mineralize aragonite found in archaeological sediments are entirely composed of aragonite, or if aragonite is present in ash, based on FTIR one can assume that the carbonates and phosphates in the same sedimentary context are well preserved, and that their distributions should also reflect their original depositional arrangements (Weiner 2010; Toffolo & Boaretto 2014).

When aragonite and calcite dissolve, they release calcium and carbonate ions in solution, which precipitate as secondary calcite upon water evaporation (assuming that ions are not transported away from the site by groundwater flow). However, if phosphate ions are present in solution, carbonate hydroxyapatite will form. Phosphates may originate from the dissolution of carbonate hydroxyapatite in bones, which starts dissolving when the pH of groundwater drops below 8 and completely disappears at pH values under 7 (Berna *et al.* 2004), or from the breakdown of organic matter, notably bird and bat guano in caves (Shahack-Gross *et al.* 2004a; Friesem *et al.* 2021b). For pH values between 8 and 7, secondary carbonate hydroxyapatite forms. At pH < 7 and high phosphate concentrations in solution, montgomeryite forms, whereas crandallite forms at low phosphate concentrations. Depending on the ions in solution and their concentrations, leucophosphite, whitlockite, and tinsleyite may form as well. Under more acidic conditions (pH ~4), the less soluble aluminum-rich phosphates variscite and taranakite form (Karkanas *et al.* 2000; Weiner 2010). These acidic conditions favor the preservation of silica, such as phytoliths, which usually dissolve in alkaline sediments (Cabanes *et al.* 2011), and charcoal (Rebollo *et al.* 2008). On the contrary, the same conditions favor the breakdown of clay minerals, which tend to react with phosphates and become less crystalline, showing band shifts similar to those observed when clay minerals are exposed to elevated temperatures (Weiner *et al.* 2002). Mapping of the spatial distribution of these minerals using FTIR and micromorphology of sediments allows tracking diagenetic processes in three dimensions throughout the stratigraphic sequence of a site, which can be used to predict whether specific minerals will be preserved at a given location (e.g., Weiner *et al.* 1993, 2002, 2007; Schiegl *et al.* 1996; Albert *et al.* 1999; Karkanas *et al.* 1999, 2002; Stiner *et al.* 2001; Weiner 2010; Berna *et al.* 2021; Friesem *et al.* 2021a). For instance, Weiner *et al.* (1993, 2002, 2007) determined that in some levels at Kebara Cave and Hayonim Cave (Israel), bones are not present because they were never deposited, and not because they dissolved. This was based on the occurrence of more soluble calcite in levels where bones were absent.

4.1.2 Crystallinity of Calcium Carbonate and Carbonate Hydroxyapatite

As described, calcite crystals undergo Ostwald ripening upon dissolution and recrystallization, and thus become more crystalline with diagenesis. These changes can be tracked using the grinding curve method and reflection FTIR microspectroscopy, especially when the starting material is pyrogenic calcite. Recently, the same phenomenon has been observed in pyrogenic aragonite. Using a combination of FTIR, SEM, and radiocarbon dating, Toffolo *et al.* (2023b) demonstrated that pyrogenic aragonite crystals found in a Middle

Bronze Age (~1600 BCE) ash layer at Tell es-Safi/Gath (Israel) grew over time to form secondary aragonite, which is characterized by a different isotopic composition and thus cannot provide accurate age determinations (see Section 4.2.1). Similarly, Toffolo (2021) showed with SEM that discolored *Glycymeris nummaria* shells from the early Iron Age (~1000 BCE) levels at Ashkelon (Israel), which based on FTIR are entirely composed of aragonite, exhibit dissolution features and secondary crystals that likely entailed isotopic exchange with the environment. Therefore, these shells cannot be used for the analysis of carbon- and oxygen-stable isotopes to extract environmental records, or to obtain absolute dates. The same may apply to aragonite shells mineralized by other species found in archaeological sediments. If a robust reference is established, FTIR grinding curves may help distinguish primary and secondary biogenic aragonite in shells. These results indicate that while the presence of aragonite shells in archaeological sediments can be regarded as a reliable proxy for the overall good preservation of the less soluble calcite and carbonate hydroxyapatite within the same context, this might not be true for the same aragonite shells in terms of isotopic composition.

Carbonate hydroxyapatite crystals in bone undergo recrystallization between pH 7 and 8, and thus become more crystalline. This process can be monitored with different types of band ratios, including the carbonate content, IRSF, and $1,060$ cm^{-1}/$1,075$ cm^{-1} (see Section 3.3.1). However, only the grinding curve method can decouple particle size from atomic order and determine different degrees of crystallinity (Asscher *et al.* 2011b; Dal Sasso *et al.* 2018). Asscher *et al.* (2011a) assessed the degree of diagenetic alteration of bones and teeth from different archaeological sites in Israel, however based on a modern reference baseline for the same taxa. Xin *et al.* (2021) determined the state of preservation of carbonate hydroxyapatite in pigeon bones from different Byzantine pigeon towers in the Negev Desert (Israel) based on the grinding curve method. In addition, using the method of Dal Sasso *et al.* (2018), they found that the relation between the IRSF and the FW85% of the ~603 cm^{-1} peak of phosphates indicates that most of the carbonate hydroxyapatite crystals are relatively small as in fresh bone and thus the specimens can be considered as well preserved. In FTIR microspectroscopy, where the grinding curve cannot be applied because samples are mounted in thin sections or polished slabs, the $1,060$ cm^{-1}/$1,075$ cm^{-1} ratio can differentiate fresh bone, dentine, cementum, and enamel, and track diagenetic changes and heat alteration in fossil bones (Lebon *et al.* 2011, 2014).

During recrystallization, bones may incorporate fluoride from groundwater, which substitutes for hydroxyl groups and leads to the formation of fluoridated carbonate hydroxyapatite. This process takes place over long periods of time and affects very old bones (e.g., Piga *et al.* 2011). Using FTIR in transmission and microspectroscopy in reflection, Toffolo *et al.* (2015) demonstrated that the formation of fluoridated carbonate hydroxyapatite in Middle Pleistocene bones found at Florisbad (South Africa) started on the outer surface of the cortical tissue, possibly due to a "wicking effect" promoted by the evaporation through capillary action of groundwater concentrated on the outer surface of bones (Trueman *et al.* 2004). Since the local thermal spring is rich in fluoride, bones from the 1930s collection, whose position was not recorded during excavation, could be linked to a small area around the spring eye based on FTIR results. Bones excavated from known locations further away from the spring eye showed progressively less fluoride incorporation.

Tooth enamel consists of carbonate hydroxyapatite as in bone mineral, although enamel crystals are much larger and more ordered at the atomic level (Weiner 2010). This makes them more resistant to dissolution and recrystallization processes compared to carbonate hydroxyapatite in bone, dentin, and cementum, but it does not mean that they do not undergo diagenesis at all. The simple fact that enamel incorporates uranium during burial, a main factor in electron spin resonance (ESR) dating (see Section 4.2.3), points to some degree of alteration. Sponheimer and Lee-Thorp (1999) showed using FTIR that there are changes in the relative distributions of carbonate groups of type A and B in fossil enamel. More recently, Asscher *et al.* (2011a) used the grinding curve method to identify altered enamel samples from archaeological sites in Israel. They also proposed a way to quantify the degree of diagenesis in enamel by subtracting the IRSF value of modern enamel from the IRSF value of the fossil specimen and dividing the result by the IRSF value of modern enamel, using as reference an arbitrary FWHM of 100 cm^{-1} for the phosphate v_3. Therefore, tooth enamel does undergo diagenesis when embedded in sediments, and this may lead to significant changes in its isotopic composition. Obviously, these changes must be considered prior to the analysis of carbon, oxygen, and strontium stable isotopes aimed at reconstructing mobility patterns, paleodiet, and paleoclimate, which may otherwise be significantly inaccurate.

4.2 Absolute Dating

The possibility to determine the composition of archaeological materials, and in some cases their state of preservation, has made FTIR spectroscopy one of the preferred methods in the screening of samples for absolute dating. Given that several dating methods are affected by small changes in the isotopic composition of samples, tracking the diagenetic path of materials is of the utmost importance in order to obtain accurate age determinations.

4.2.1 Radiocarbon Dating

Bone collagen and wood charcoal are the main materials used in radiocarbon dating, which measures the amount of radiocarbon in organic and inorganic materials up to 50,000 years old (Bowman 1990). However, both collagen and charcoal tend to degrade when embedded in sediments, to the point where they cannot produce reliable age determinations (Weiner 2010). This is often verified as a result of expensive laboratory procedures aimed at extracting collagen from bones and purifying charcoal, which also determine the partial or complete destruction of valuable archaeological material. Fourier transform infrared spectroscopy proved an invaluable and rapid method in the screening of samples prior to dating (e.g., Boaretto 2008, 2009). For instance, Yizhaq *et al.* (2005) selected bones from the Pre-Pottery Neolithic B (PPNB) site of Motza (Israel) for radiocarbon dating based on the occurrence of collagen diagnostic bands (amide I–II, proline) in the insoluble fraction of weighted aliquots of bone powder dissolved in 1 M HCl. Results were confirmed by the measurement of C:N ratios using an elemental analyzer. In the case of fairly well-preserved bones, collagen bands may be identified by performing FTIR directly on the bone powder in transmission mode (e.g., Toffolo *et al.* 2013a; Xin *et al.* 2021; Rhodes *et al.* 2022), or on bone fragments in ATR (e.g., Pothier Bouchard *et al.* 2019). The amount of collagen can also be estimated by calculating the ratio of the amide I and phosphate v_3 bands (e.g., Trueman *et al.* 2004; Lebon *et al.* 2016).

Yizhaq *et al.* (2005) also found that charcoal tends to degrade after the acid-alkali-acid (AAA) treatment aimed at removing contaminants such as humic acids, as indicated by the increase in intensity of the Si–O–Si band of clay minerals and the decrease of the fossil charcoal bands between 1,718 and 1,595 cm^{-1}. Cohen-Ofri *et al.* (2006) showed that graphite-like crystallites decrease in fossil charcoal compared to fresh charcoal, whereas non-organized structures (i.e., non-diffracting) increase, as well as carboxylate groups. Thus, charcoal becomes more soluble, especially under high pH conditions, and resembles humic substances from the soil, making it more difficult to separate the two and obtain accurate age determinations. At the same time, loss of charcoal may result in the uptake of clay minerals containing adsorbed organics of unknown origin. Rebollo *et al.* (2008) showed how each stage of the AAA treatment disrupts the charcoal structure, especially in extensively degraded samples, and suggested using FTIR to check the integrity of the sample after each step. Therefore, charcoal samples that are rich in clay minerals even before the AAA treatment, based on FTIR spectra, should be selected with caution (e.g., Boaretto *et al.* 2009; Rebollo *et al.* 2011; Boaretto *et al.* 2021).

Screening of samples with FTIR is a fundamental step also in radiocarbon dating of $CaCO_3$, a major carbon-bearing material in its different forms. For instance, mollusk shells are another common radiocarbon dating material that requires phase identification prior to dating. Several species mineralize aragonite shells, and as we have seen this mineral is prone to dissolution and recrystallization into calcite when embedded in archaeological sediments under unfavorable chemical environments; the same applies to fish otoliths, which are made of aragonite (Weiner 2010; Toffolo 2021 and references therein). Therefore, FTIR can determine whether samples include secondary calcite, which should be avoided for radiocarbon dating due to its likely altered isotopic composition. Barbieri *et al.* (2018) used FTIR to determine the composition of land snail shells extracted from cores collected in the Ach Valley of the Swabian Jura (Germany), which were entirely composed of aragonite, and for that reason were targeted for dating.

Wood ash, lime plaster, and lime mortar are materials made of $CaCO_3$, mainly in the form of pyrogenic calcite but often mixed with pyrogenic and/ or biogenic aragonite, geogenic and/or biogenic calcite, dolomite, portlandite, hydromagnesite, pozzolana, quartz, clay minerals, and layered double hydroxides (e.g., Regev *et al.* 2010b, 2011; Boaretto & Poduska 2013; Toffolo & Boaretto 2014; Toffolo *et al.* 2017b, 2017c, 2019a, 2020a; Urbanová *et al.* 2020; Toffolo *et al.* 2023b). Wood ash forms when calcium oxalate in wood turns to calcite at temperatures above 400 °C, and this form is loosely referred to as "low-temperature ash." This pyrogenic calcite may share the same isotopic composition as the cellulose of the plant that mineralized the oxalates, although this is not always the case and for this reason radiocarbon dating of low-temperature ash may succeed only if a number of conditions are satisfied (Regev *et al.* 2011). If the temperature of the fire exceeds 600 °C, calcite turns into CaO. This phase is unstable at ambient conditions, and when the fire is extinguished it reacts with atmospheric humidity to form $Ca(OH)_2$, which subsequently turns into $CaCO_3$ upon incorporation of CO_2. This is usually called "high-temperature ash." A similar process takes place in the production of lime plaster, which starts with the burning of limestone or chalk to temperatures above 800 °C. This produces CaO, which is later mixed with water to obtain $Ca(OH)_2$ and eventually $CaCO_3$. Both high-temperature ash and lime plaster are mainly composed of pyrogenic calcite but sometimes may include pyrogenic aragonite. Upon carbonation, $Ca(OH)_2$ incorporates ^{14}C from the atmosphere, thus making both high-temperature ash and lime plaster/mortar suitable materials for radiocarbon dating (Toffolo 2020 and references therein). Unfortunately, $CaCO_3$ is a soluble mineral in sediments and thus tends to dissolve and reprecipitate when the pH drops under 8 (Weiner 2010). In solution, $CaCO_3$ exchanges carbon, which may derive from different sources, both radiocarbon-free (geologic) and recent. In addition, mixing of $Ca(OH)_2$ with geogenic calcite in lime plaster/mortar introduces contamination from "dead carbon." This mixed signature, if dated by radiocarbon, provides inaccurate ages.

In order to target the unaltered pyrogenic $CaCO_3$ crystals, which are supposed to represent the time of formation of the material, the grinding curve method is first applied to assess the state of preservation of crystals in bulk samples (Toffolo 2020). Spatially resolved information may be obtained using FTIR microspectroscopy. Poduska *et al.* (2012) identified the best-preserved samples of PPNB lime plaster from Yiftahel (Israel) based on the position and width of the v_3 band of calcite, which is sharp and located at ~1,410 cm^{-1} in unaltered plaster; these samples were then targeted for radiocarbon dating. If the degree of atomic order of the sample is consistent with that of experimental lime plaster, or similar to that, the most disordered $CaCO_3$ crystals may be separated from the rest of the sample based on density. The latter is lower in pyrogenic $CaCO_3$ compared to its geogenic counterpart (Toffolo *et al.* 2020a). Given the low efficiency of the separation by density, the degree of atomic order of the lighter crystals is verified again using the grinding curve method, and if it overlaps with experimental lime plaster, the sample is heated in vacuum to 500 °C to release the CO_2 necessary for dating. This approach was successfully applied to aragonite-rich ash at Iron Age Megiddo (Toffolo *et al.* 2017b) and calcite lime plaster at Byzantine Shivta (Toffolo *et al.* 2020a), both located in Israel. At Middle Bronze Age Tell es-Safi/Gath (Israel), a combination of FTIR, micro-FTIR, scanning electron microscopy, and radiocarbon dating determined that a large proportion of an aragonite-rich ash layer is actually composed of secondary aragonite crystals, which cannot be accurately dated due to post-depositional exchange with geogenic carbon (Toffolo *et al.* 2023b).

4.2.2 Uranium Series Dating

Uranium series (U-series) dating is based on the decay chains of uranium found in $CaCO_3$ materials such as corals and speleothems. In particular, the U-Th method, based on the decay of ^{234}U to ^{230}Th within the ^{238}U decay chain, rests on the assumption that the dated materials are closed systems, that is, they do not exchange uranium or thorium with the environment after their formation (Pons-Branchu 2023). This condition is not always satisfied in corals and speleothems. These materials, which are composed of aragonite or calcite, tend to dissolve and reprecipitate as secondary aragonite and/or secondary calcite. When primary aragonite turns into secondary calcite, this process leads to uranium loss compared to the parent material, and thus age overestimation, because the large aragonite CaO_9 polyhedron is better suited to accommodating large cations such as UO_2^{2+} (uranyl), compared with the smaller CaO_6 octahedron of calcite (Toffolo 2021 and references therein). Fourier transform infrared spectroscopy can provide a screening method to select primary aragonite crystals for U-series. Pons-Branchu *et al.* (2022) used FTIR microspectroscopy to map aragonite in Holocene speleothems from Nerja Cave (Spain). Aragonite was then cross-dated using radiocarbon and U-series, providing the only consistent age determinations between the two methods, as opposed to calcite, with further implications for the dating of Paleolithic rock art in caves.

4.2.3 Electron Spin Resonance Dating

Electron spin resonance dating of teeth is based on the measurement of the energy stored by carbonate hydroxyapatite crystals in enamel during burial. The radiation coming from cosmic rays and the radioactive decay of natural isotopes such as uranium, thorium, and potassium ionizes the material leading to the trapping of electrons in defects in the crystal lattice. U, Th, and K are present in the sedimentary matrix in which the tooth is embedded, and the dental tissues (enamel, dentine, and cement) incorporate U during burial. The dose of energy absorbed by carbonate hydroxyapatite crystals (called the "equivalent dose") is quantified using ESR spectrometry, whereas the annual dose received from the environment and from the tooth itself (called the "dose rate") is measured mainly using gamma spectrometry and/or mass spectrometry. The ratio between equivalent dose and dose rate provides the age of the sample (Richard 2023). The main assumption of ESR dating is that the dose rate is constant through time; however, that actually depends on the kinetics of incorporation of radioactive isotopes in the dental tissues, especially uranium that is soluble in water. In addition, the formation of diagenetic minerals rich in radioactive isotopes, for instance authigenic phosphates containing ^{40}K derived from the dissolution of wood ash layers from different locations at the site, can alter the dose rate in the sedimentary matrix around the tooth at any given time after burial. This phenomenon has been recognized as a possible source of inaccuracy both for ESR and thermoluminescence dating at Hayomim Cave (Israel), where Mercier *et al.* (1995, 2007) and Rink *et al.* (2004) used FTIR to track the diagenesis of the sedimentary matrix around heated flints and teeth selected for dating, respectively. Enamel *in vivo* does not contain uranium; incorporation occurs during the recrystallization process of hydroxyapatite crystals, which become larger and more ordered. Since dental tissues do undergo diagenesis in sediments (e.g., Dauphin *et al.* 2018), the dose rate, and thus the uptake of uranium through time, needs to be modeled using U-series (Grün *et al.* 1988). Unfortunately, uranium uptake modeling cannot be applied to samples affected by uranium leaching during burial, which is detected when at least one of the dental tissues exhibits a U-series age greater than the ESR age that accounts for an early uptake of uranium (i.e., soon after deposition in sediments). This is due to the fact that it is not possible to quantify how much uranium, which contributed to the dose rate while in the enamel, may have been lost over time. As is the case in radiocarbon dating of bone collagen, uranium leaching is detected after ESR and U-series dating, which imply lengthy and expensive laboratory procedures. Richard *et al.* (2022, 2023) found a positive correlation between increased degree of atomic order and uranium content of fossil enamel in the teeth of small antelopes, possibly the extinct springbok *Antidorcas bondi*, recovered at the Middle Stone Age site of Lovedale (South Africa). Using the grinding curve method of Asscher *et al.* (2011a, 2011b) for carbonate hydroxyapatite, the authors showed that the most crystalline samples of enamel (compared to a modern reference of *A. marsupialis*) are also the richest in uranium, which was incorporated during diagenesis. Based on ESR and U-series results, the same samples may have suffered uranium leaching, which must have taken place during the same diagenetic processes. Therefore, this method allows to screen enamel samples and discard the well-crystallized ones, which are the most likely candidates for both uranium uptake and leaching. The authors also showed that there is a correlation between uranium content and laser-induced fluorescence (LIF) of the enamel, which, in the two samples richer in uranium, exhibits emissions consistent with uranyl. Since LIF is a non-destructive method, it could well be used to screen rare and precious specimens, such as human teeth.

4.3 Pyrotechnology

The field of ancient pyrotechnology research has greatly benefited from the application of FTIR spectroscopy to the analysis of archaeological sediments and materials, especially in the identification of combustion features, heat-treated raw materials for stone tool manufacture, and the production of lime plaster and mortar.

4.3.1 Combustion Features

The possibility to detect by FTIR heat-altered clay minerals and pyrogenic $CaCO_3$, which together with charcoal are the most common byproducts of the combustion of wood on a sediment substrate, has greatly facilitated the identification of combustion features, especially when these are not structured and thus difficult to recognize by simply observing sediments (Weiner 2010; Mentzer

2014; Goldberg *et al.* 2017). Based on the work by van der Marel & Beutelspacher (1976) on standard materials, by Shoval (1993, 1994) on a Persian pottery kiln at Tel Michal (Israel), by Karkanas *et al.* (2004) on Upper Paleolithic clay hearths from Klissoura Cave (Greece), and by Berna *et al.* (2007) on Bronze and Iron Age combustion features at Tel Dor (Israel), which showed how exposure to temperatures above ~400 °C leads to the disappearance and shift of different bands of clay minerals, heat alteration has been identified using FTIR spectroscopy and microspectroscopy at several archaeological sites across the globe spanning the last 300,000 years (e.g., Berna & Goldberg 2008; Eliyahu-Behar *et al.* 2008; Cabanes *et al.* 2010; Mallol *et al.* 2010; Namdar *et al.* 2011; Aldeias *et al.* 2012; Berna *et al.* 2012; Shahack-Gross *et al.* 2014; Villagran *et al.* 2017; Patania *et al.* 2019; Esteban *et al.* 2020; Grono *et al.* 2022; Toffolo *et al.* 2023c). With the improvements proposed by Forget *et al.* (2015) with regard to combustion atmosphere, and by Ogloblin Ramírez *et al.* (2023) on the effects of mixing heated and unheated clay minerals, the interpretation of spectra of purported combustion features has become more robust. Similarly, the grinding curve method has allowed the identification of pyrogenic $CaCO_3$ in the form of ash (e.g., Cabanes *et al.* 2012; Toffolo *et al.* 2012; Eliyahu-Behar *et al.* 2012; Asscher *et al.* 2015; Regev *et al.* 2015; Eliyahu-Behar *et al.* 2017a; Esteban *et al.* 2018; Toffolo *et al.* 2018; Burguet-Coca *et al.* 2020; Weiner *et al.* 2020; Shalom *et al.* 2023; Alonso-Eguiluz *et al.* 2024). Pyrogenic calcite crystals may be mixed with geogenic calcite in some types of sedimentary matrices, such as loess and *terra rossa*, and thus yield an unclear FTIR signal. In these cases, micromorphology thin sections can aid the identification of pyrogenic crystals (e.g., Poduska *et al.* 2012; Friesem *et al.* 2014; Mentzer 2014; Shahack-Gross *et al.* 2014). Besides these components, burnt bone has been used as a proxy for combustion, and in particular the 630 cm^{-1} band of carbonate hydroxyapatite exposed to temperatures exceeding 500 °C (e.g., Stiner *et al.* 1995; Schiegl *et al.* 2003; Berna *et al.* 2012; Walker *et al.* 2016; Toffolo *et al.* 2017b; Larbey *et al.* 2019; Patania *et al.* 2019; Villagran *et al.* 2021; Stepka *et al.* 2022; Toffolo *et al.* 2023b). In some cases, the simple occurrence of minerals that are known to form only through high-temperature burning is enough to determine the presence of a combustion feature. These include pyrogenic aragonite, cristobalite, tridymite, and glass (e.g., Toffolo & Boaretto 2014; Eliyahu-Behar *et al.* 2017b; Toffolo *et al.* 2017b; Weiner *et al.* 2020; Grono *et al.* 2022; Fernández-Palacios *et al.* 2023; Shalom *et al.* 2023; Toffolo *et al.* 2023b). In other cases, the absence of biogenic aragonite where it should be preserved is used as a proxy for exposure to high temperatures, since aragonite turns into calcite above ~300 °C (e.g., Yoshioka & Kitano 1985; Aldeias *et al.* 2019). Simões and Aldeias (2022) used FTIR microspectroscopy of micromorphology thin sections to map the occurrence of calcite, and thus *in-situ* heating, at the Cabeço da Amoreira and Poças de São Bento Mesolithic shell middens in Portugal, which include species that mineralize aragonite. At the Kolonna site in Greece, Karkanas *et al.* (2019) showed with FTIR microspectroscopy of micromorphology thin sections that the aragonitic oolites in the construction material of a Late Bronze Age updraft pottery kiln turned to calcite in its floor and inside walls, indicating that they were exposed to elevated temperatures. The two polymorphs were differentiated in transmission based on the different shape of the calcite $v_1 + v_3$ band at ~2,513 cm^{-1}, which in aragonite is a triplet with a peak at ~2,530 cm^{-1}.

One of the most important contributions of FTIR with regard to the identification of combustion features is in the study of the origin of controlled use of fire by the genus *Homo*, a major technological advancement that had enormous implications in the biological and cultural evolution of humans (Sandgathe & Berna 2017). Currently, the earliest evidence dates back to approximately 1 Ma and was found in the Acheulean levels at Wonderwerk Cave in South Africa, where Berna *et al.* (2012) identified burnt bone using FTIR spectroscopy of bone fragments and FTIR microspectroscopy on micromorphology thin sections of ash deposits. This was later confirmed by Thibodeau (2016), who identified ashed plant fibers in thin sections based on the width of the v_3 of calcite at 75 percent of its intensity in reflection spectra. Similar results were obtained by Stepka *et al.* (2022) from the analysis of bone fragments recovered at the Evron Quarry site in Israel, dated to 1–0.8 Ma, although the open-air nature of the site keeps open the possibility of wildfires. Transmission FTIR on bones from Locality 1 (~500–200 ka) at Zhoukoudian, China, showed that only a few specimens are burned, possibly as a result of natural causes; integration of micromorphological analysis demonstrated that no combustion features are present (Weiner *et al.* 1998). Similarly, FTIR microspectroscopy of micromorphology thin sections excluded the occurrence of combustion features at the Lower Paleolithic site of Schöningen in Germany (Stahlschmidt *et al.* 2015). On the contrary, the same approach produced the evidence for the repeated use of a central hearth dated to ~300 ka at Qesem Cave in Israel, based on the occurrence of burnt bones and aggregates of heated clay minerals (Karkanas *et al.* 2007; Shahack-Gross *et al.* 2014).

4.3.2 Heat Treatment of Lithic Raw Materials

Besides the possibility to cook foods, produce light and warmth, and provide a means of defense, controlled use of fire allowed the development of pyrotechnological production activities, the first of which was probably the heat treatment of lithic raw materials. This practice improves the fracture quality of some types of silicate rocks, such as flint (cryptocrystalline quartz) and silcrete (soil crust cemented by silica), which are among the most exploited raw materials during the Paleolithic in Eurasia and the Stone Age in Africa. The earliest evidence of lithic heat treatment was found at Hoedjiespunt 1, a Middle Stone Age site in South Africa dated to ~130–119 ka where silcrete was systematically heated (Schmidt *et al.* 2020). Upon exposure to elevated temperatures, both flint and silcrete undergo structural changes that affect the coherence of cryptocrystalline quartz grains. These are composed of bridging Si–O–Si bonds interrupted by chemically bound hydroxyl groups forming silanol groups (SiOH). Starting from 250 ºC, silanols are lost and new Si–O–Si bonds are formed, resulting in decreased fracture toughness and thus better control over fracture and improved edge sharpness, notably in the case of pressure flaking (Brown *et al.* 2009; Mourre *et al.* 2010; Schmidt & Frölich 2011; Schmidt *et al.* 2011, 2012, 2013b).

The loss of silanols upon exposure to elevated temperatures has been monitored using FTIR spectroscopy in both flint and silcrete using reflectance in the NIR range (Schmidt & Frölich 2011; Schmidt *et al.* 2011, 2012, 2013b). With regard to the MIR range, Schmidt and Frölich (2011) showed that that the 555 cm^{-1} band of chalcedony, which represents the silanols, loses intensity with heat, a process that starts already at 250 ºC and that leads to the disappearance of the band between 450 and 600 ºC. Therefore, this band can be used as a proxy for heat treatment. However, not all flints contain silanol groups. Weiner *et al.* (2015) developed a different approach to analyze flints from Manot Cave (Israel), in which the silanol band at 555 cm^{-1} was very weak or absent. The authors observed that the intensity of the ~512 cm^{-1} band of quartz (Si–O bending) in natural flint nodules from the cave wall decreases with increasing temperature. In addition, the ~512 and ~467 cm^{-1} bands become broader above 500 ºC, presumably due to increasing atomic disorder induced by heat. To quantify this phenomenon, they calculated the ratio between the intensity of the ~512 cm^{-1} band and the intensity of the valley between this band and the adjacent ~467 cm^{-1} band (using a baseline between 600 and 410 cm^{-1}), and showed that the ratio starts decreasing between 200 and 400 ºC depending on the source location. A combination of the two methods is the best approach to determine whether archaeological flint was heat-treated.

4.3.3 Lime Plaster Production

As outlined in Section 4.2.1, lime plaster is produced by heating carbonate rocks (limestone, chalk, marble, travertine, dolostone, etc.) to temperatures exceeding 800 ºC to obtain quicklime, which is then mixed with water to produce hydrated lime. The latter is a moldable putty used in construction as coating or binder, for example, mixed with sand and placed between courses of cobbles/bricks. Upon drying, lime plaster/mortar hardens, and at the mineralogical level it turns back to $CaCO_3$ (Weiner 2010). As we have seen, since the degree of atomic order of calcite in lime plaster is much lower compared to that of geogenic calcite, the former can be identified in archaeological materials and sediments using the grinding curve method in transmission mode (Regev *et al.* 2010a; Poduska *et al.* 2011). Using FTIR microspectroscopy in reflection mode, the degree of atomic order of calcite in lime plaster can be determined based on the position and shape of the v_3 band (Poduska *et al.* 2012).

Lime plaster is among the first pyrotechnological materials produced by humans, as shown by SEM and XRD analyses of early binders recovered at the Lagama North VIII site in Sinai (Egypt), dated to the Epipaleolithic (~16 ka), where lime plaster was used as adhesive on the ventral surface of Geometric Kebaran microliths (Kingery *et al.* 1988 and references therein). Small-scale production of lime plaster emerged in the Natufian culture of southwestern Asia, at the transition between Epipaleolithic and Neolithic, when quicklime was obtained presumably by burning chunks of limestone in hearths. This type of production process was described in the Early Natufian (~14 ka) deposits at Hayonim Cave in Israel (Kingery *et al.* 1988 and references therein), where Chu *et al.* (2008) used the v_2/v_4 ratio to show that the calcite from a large hearth is indeed consistent with experimental lime plaster. The same method was used to characterize lime plasters from Early Natufian graves at Eynan in Israel (Valla *et al.* 2007; Chu *et al.* 2008). More recently, Friesem *et al.* (2019) used the grinding curve method to show that high-purity (i.e., not mixed with additives) lime plaster was used to cover a grave at the Late Natufian (~12 ka) site of Nahal Ein Gev II (Israel).

Lime plaster production attained a much larger scale with the onset of the PPNB period (starting ~10.4 ka), when lime plaster was used to coat large surface extents of floors and walls, besides graves and buried human skulls, and its use expanded in southwestern Asia. The greater volumes of quicklime produced in this period required more effective installations, such as sunken lime kilns (Kingery *et al.* 1988). One such example was found at the early PPNB site of Nesher Ramla Quarry (Israel), where a shallow karst sinkhole was filled up with sediment and stacked limestone cobbles (Ullman *et al.* 2022). Using a combination of FTIR in transmission and FTIR microspectroscopy in transmission (for clay minerals) and reflection (for calcite) modes, Toffolo *et al.* (2017c) identified *in-situ* combustion features, fragments of lime plaster, and heated sediments displaced by the recovery of quicklime in the sinkhole.

Poduska *et al.* (2012) determined the state of preservation of different layers of lime plaster floors at Yiftahel (Israel) using the grinding curve method on bulk samples and FTIR microspectroscopy on petrographic thin sections. Their findings demonstrate that only the top-most thin coat of lime plaster was pure, whereas the base was mixed with chunks of unheated limestone used as filler. Similar construction methods have been documented at PPNB Motza (Israel), although the plasters exhibit slight differences in composition. Toffolo *et al.* (2019a) showed with FTIR grinding curves and XRD that some of the plasters from Motza include more than 20 percent pyrogenic aragonite, and thus should be regarded as well preserved and potentially suitable for radiocarbon dating. Maor *et al.* (2023) detected the presence of dolomite, especially in the preparation layers as dolostone was a locally available material, and developed reference grinding curves of experimental calcite–dolomite mixtures to assess the degree of atomic order of calcite in mixed plasters, and therefore their state of preservation. Based on these results, and published micromorphological analyses of PPNB lime plasters from various sites in Israel, Friesem *et al.* (2019) convincingly argued that the addition of limestone, dolostone, clay, dung, and plant fibers to the hydrated lime putty reflects a technological advancement in the production of lime plaster during the PPNB, aimed at increasing its durability and saving on quicklime. Starting from the Bronze Age, lime plaster became widespread in the Mediterranean basin and its occurrence has been documented at a number of sites using the grinding curve method (e.g., Regev *et al.* 2010b, 2015; Goshen *et al.* 2017; Amadio 2018; Amadio *et al.* 2020; Asscher *et al.* 2020; Toffolo *et al.* 2020a; Calandra *et al.* 2022).

Lime plaster technology was developed also in other parts of the world, and in recent years FTIR has been applied to the characterization of kilns and lime plaster floors. Grono *et al.* (2022) used the grinding curve method and the presence of pyrogenic aragonite to identify lime plaster floors at the Neolithic (~3,500 cal. BP) site of Loc Giang in southern Vietnam. Ortiz Ruiz *et al.* (2023) used FTIR in ATR mode to track the exposure to high temperatures of the sediments filling a Maya lime kiln at Dzibilchaltún (Mexico), based on the area ratio of the v_2 and v_4 bands of calcite in samples where the FWHM of the v_3 ranges between 110 and 130 cm^{-1}. Although there is less control over particle size compared to the grinding curves in transmission, this method consistently differentiates the local limestone from lime plaster, including temperature differences in quicklime production above 750 ºC.

5 Concluding Perspective

FTIR spectroscopy is widely used to reconstruct site formation and post-depositional processes, determine the occurrence of combustion features and materials related to human use of fire, and understand the degree of preservation of materials used for absolute dating and paleoenvironmental studies. The recent advancement of the grinding curve method allowed to solve the problem of separating the opposite effects of particle size and atomic order on the shape of infrared spectra, thus providing invaluable insights into the diagenetic history of the minerals that make up many materials of archaeological significance. It can be predicted that in the future, this method will be applied to more materials made of calcite, aragonite, carbonate hydroxyapatite, or quartz. For instance, if changes in the infrared spectrum of cryptocrystalline quartz have been observed in flints exposed to elevated temperatures, other changes may be observed as a result of diagenetic processes, similar to what happens in clay minerals. With regard to calcite and aragonite, a larger range of biogenic materials may be probed. The grinding curve method showed differences in the degree of atomic order of different tissues of the same species, such as in sea urchins and marine bivalve mollusks (Regev *et al.* 2010a; Suzuki *et al.* 2011). This may turn out to be also the case of avian eggshells, which are known to be "protected niches" able to preserve DNA (Oskam *et al.* 2010; Weiner 2010), and have been used as markers of prehistoric social networks based on their elemental composition (Stewart *et al.* 2020). Similarly, the preservation of ancient DNA in sediments has been shown to depend on the mineralogy of the context, with carbonate hydroxyapatite and calcite exhibiting the greatest chemical affinity for DNA (Massilani *et al.* 2022; Freeman *et al.* 2023). In the case of calcite and carbonate hydroxyapatite, for instance, tracking diagenetic paths is of fundamental importance given their high solubility in sedimentary contexts where groundwater pH drops below 8. Dissolution of DNA-bearing crystals in wood ash and bones may lead to their re-precipitation as secondary minerals in contexts that formed under different environmental conditions and at markedly different times compared to the parent material. This becomes especially apparent in open sedimentary systems and in caves, where groundwater movement by gravity or capillary action can significantly alter the geochemistry of the deposits. As a result, the accuracy of the correlation between DNA and other proxies extracted from sediments (phytoliths, pollen, diatoms, enamel stable isotopes, leaf wax biomarkers, silicates for luminescence dating, etc.) may be drastically lowered or entirely compromised. Therefore, thorough characterization of the sedimentary context is a necessary starting condition for parsimonious interpretations of the sedimentary DNA record. The grinding curve method and the broadening of the carbonate v_3 in FTIR microspectroscopy can help distinguish primary and secondary crystals and thus increase the accuracy of analyses that target these minerals.

The issue of determining the state of preservation of minerals in archaeological sediments and materials is so crucial for a correct interpretation of the archaeological record that a recent trend has emerged, which involves the use of other methods to assess the degree of atomic order of minerals alongside FTIR (Toffolo 2018). Xu *et al.* (2015, 2016) explored defects in the crystal lattice of calcite using XRD and X-ray absorption spectroscopy, and these in turn affect grinding curves. Using FTIR grinding curves of calcite and aragonite standard materials as a reference benchmark, recent studies have shown that other types of spectroscopy can effectively distinguish geogenic and pyrogenic materials. Toffolo *et al.* (2019b, 2020b) used scanning electron microscopy coupled with cathodoluminescence (SEM-CL), and LIF to identify well-preserved lime plaster, as opposed to recrystallized plaster and limestone/chalk. The former exhibits blue CL, which is produced by structural defects in the crystal lattice, similar to the defects that determine the atomic disorder probed with the grinding curves. Recrystallized plaster exhibits more orange-red CL, which is caused by manganese ions substituting for calcium in the $CaCO_3$ lattice. Limestone and chalk, on the contrary, are characterized by orange-red CL as a result of their formation process. A similar trend was observed with LIF, which has also been used to identify recrystallized carbonate hydroxyapatite in fossil enamel, based on presence of emissions produced by uranyl (Richard *et al.* 2022). Furthermore, Toffolo *et al.* (2023a) probed the degree of atomic order of calcite using Raman microspectroscopy on bulk samples and thin sections. Materials that are inherently disordered, such as lime plaster, are consistently characterized by a broader Raman v_1 band $(1{,}087 \text{ cm}^{-1})$, whereas geogenic materials exhibit much narrower bands. All these methods have the added advantage of being nondestructive, a major requirement for some types of archaeological materials. It can be envisaged that more methods will provide independent lines of evidence that can inform on the degree of atomic order of minerals, in combination with FTIR.

Obviously, some of these advancements require the use of microscopy in order to analyze single crystals or aggregates of crystals. The insights obtained from chemical maps generated through FTIR microspectroscopy are of enormous importance, but depend on the development of statistical tools necessary to analyze large datasets. Thibodeau (2016) showed the potential of statistics applied to chemical maps in order to retrieve spatially resolved information on the occurrence of pyrogenic calcite. Machine learning is currently being applied to the analysis of specific phases in large datasets of infrared spectra, such as bone collagen (Chowdhury *et al.* 2021). Similar results have been obtained using Raman spectra of heated flint (e.g., Stepka *et al.* 2022), and could be extended to FTIR and to the analysis of chemical maps. This approach has the potential to automatize library search of complex mixtures, and to standardize screening systems regardless of instrumentation.

References

Addadi, L., Raz, S., Weiner, S. (2003). Taking advantage of disorder: Amorphous calcium carbonate and its roles in biomineralization. *Advanced Materials*, **15 (12)**, **959–70**. https://doi.org/10.1002/adma.200300381.

Akyuz, T., Akyuz, S., Gulec, A. (2015). Elemental and spectroscopic characterization of plasters from Fatih Mosque-Istanbul (Turkey) by combined micro-Raman, FTIR and EDXRF techniques. *Spectrochimica Acta Part A: Molecular and Biomolecular Spectroscopy*, **149**, **744–50**. https://doi.org/10.1016/j.saa.2015.05.015.

Albert, R. M., Lavi, O., Estroff, L, *et al.* (1999). Mode of occupation of Tabun Cave, Mt Carmel, Israel during the Mousterian period: A study of the sediments and phytoliths. *Journal of Archaeological Science*, **26(10)**, **1249–60**. https://doi.org/10.1006/jasc.1999.0355.

Aldeias, V., Dibble, H. L., Sandgathe, D., *et al.* (2016). How heat alters underlying deposits and implications for archaeological fire features: A controlled experiment. *Journal of Archaeological Science*, **67**, **64–79**. https://doi.org/10.1016/j.jas.2016.01.016.

Aldeias, V., Goldberg, P., Sandgathe, D., *et al.* (2012). Evidence for Neandertal use of fire at Roc de Marsal (France). *Journal of Archaeological Science*, **39**, **2414–23**. https://doi.org/10.1016/j.jas.2012.01.039.

Aldeias, V., Gur-Arieh, S., Maria, R., *et al.* (2019). *Shell* we cook it? An experimental approach to the microarchaeological record of shellfish roasting. *Archaeological and Anthropological Sciences*, **11**, **389–407**. https://doi.org/10.1007/s12520-016-0413-1.

Alonso-Eguiluz, M., Toffolo, M. B., White, C. E., *et al.* (2024). The early upper paleolithic deposit of Mughr el-Hamamah (Jordan): Archaeobotanical taphonomy and site formation processes. *Journal of Archaeological Science: Reports*, **55**, **104471**. https://doi.org/10.1016/j.jasrep.2024.104471.

Amadio, M. (2018). From deposits to social practices: Integrated micromorphological analysis of floor sequences at Middle Bronze Age Erimi-*Laonin tou Porakou*, Cyprus. *Journal of Archaeological Science: Reports*, **21**, **433–49**. https://doi.org/10.1016/j.jasrep.2018.07.023.

Amadio, M., Boaretto, E., Bombardieri, L. (2020). Abandonment practices through the microscope lens. Microarchaeological data from Middle Bronze Age Erimi, Cyprus. *Levant*, **52(3)**, **301–20**. https://doi.org/10.1080/00755914.2021.1890400.

Angelini, I., Bellintani, P. (2005). Archaeological ambers from northern Italy: An FTIR-DRIFT study of provenance by comparison with the geological amber database. *Archaeometry*, **47(2)**, **441–54**. https://doi.org/10.1111/j.1475-4754.2005.00212.x.

Asscher, Y., Dal Sasso, G., Nodari, L., *et al.* (2017). Differentiating between long and short range disorder in infra-red spectra: On the meaning of "crystallinity" in silica. *Physical Chemistry Chemical Physics*, **19**, **21783–90**. https://doi.org/10.1039/C7CP03446F.

Asscher, Y., Lehmann, G., Rosen, S. A., *et al.* (2015). Absolute dating of the Late Bronze to Iron Age transition and the appearance of Philistine culture in Qubur el-Walaydah, southern Levant. *Radiocarbon*, **57(1)**, **77–97**. https://doi.org/10.2458/azu_rc.57.16961.

Asscher, Y., Regev, L., Weiner, S., *et al.* (2011a). Atomic disorder in fossil tooth and bone mineral: An FTIR study using the grinding curve method. *ArcheoSciences*, **35**, **135–41**. https://doi.org/10.4000/archeosciences.3062.

Asscher, Y., van Zuiden, A., Elimelech, C., *et al.* (2020). Prescreening hydraulic lime-binders for disordered calcite in Caesarea Maritima: Characterizing the chemical environment using FTIR. *Radiocarbon*, **62(3)**, **527–43**. https://doi.org/10.1017/RDC.2020.20.

Asscher, Y., Weiner, S., Boaretto, E. (2011b). Variations in atomic disorder in biogenic carbonate hydroxyapatite using the infrared spectrum grinding curve method. *Advanced Functional Materials*, **21**, **3308–13**. https://doi.org/10.1002/adfm.201100266.

Aufort, J., Ségalen, L., Gervais, C., *et al.* (2016). Modeling the attenuated total reflectance infrared (ATR-FTIR) spectrum of apatite. *Physics and Chemistry of Minerals*, **43**, **615–26**. https://doi.org/10.1007/s00269-016-0821-x.

Barbieri, A., Leven, C., Toffolo, M. B., *et al.* (2018). Bridging prehistoric caves with buried landscapes in the Swabian Jura (southwestern Germany). *Quaternary International*, **485**, **23–43**. https://doi.org/10.1016/j.quaint.2017.08.002.

Beasley, M. M., Bartelink, E. J., Taylor, L., Miller, R. M. (2014). Comparison of transmission FTIR, ATR, and DRIFT spectra: Implications for assessment of bone bioapatite diagenesis. *Journal of Archaeological Science*, **46**, **16–22**. https://doi.org/10.1016/j.jas.2014.03.008.

Beniash, E., Aizenberg, J., Addadi, L., *et al.* (1997). Amorphous calcium carbonate transforms into calcite during sea urchin larval spicule growth. *Proceedings of the Royal Society of London B*, **264(1380)**, **461–5**. https://doi.org/10.1098/rspb.1997.0066.

Bergamonti, L., Cirlini, M., Graiff, C., *et al.* (2022). Characterization of waxes in the Roman wall paintings of the Herculaneum Site (Italy). *Applied Sciences*, **12**, **11264**. https://doi.org/10.3390/app122111264.

Berna, F. (2017). FTIR Microscopy. In Nicosia, C., Stoops, G., eds., *Archaeological Soil and Sediment Micromorphology*. Chichester: John Wiley, pp. **411–5**. https://doi.org/10.1002/9781118941065.ch39.

Berna, F., Behar, A., Shahack-Gross, R., *et al.* (2007). Sediments exposed to high temperatures: Reconstructing pyrotechnological processes in Late Bronze and Iron Age Strata at Tel Dor (Israel). *Journal of Archaeological Science*, **34**, **358–73**. https://doi.org/10.1016/j.jas.2006.05.011.

Berna, F., Boaretto, E., Wiebe, M. C., *et al.* (2021). Site formation processes at Manot Cave, Israel: Interplay between strata accumulation in the occupation area and the talus. *Journal of Human Evolution*, **160**, **102883**. https://doi.org/10.1016/j.jhevol.2020.102883.

Berna, F., Goldberg, P. (2008). Assessing Paleolithic pyrotechnology and associated hominin behavior in Israel. *Israel Journal of Earth Sciences*, **56**, **107–21**.

Berna, F., Goldberg, P., Horwitz, L. K., *et al.* (2012). Microstratigraphic evidence of in situ fire in the Acheulean strata of Wonderwerk Cave, Northern Cape province, South Africa. *Proceedings of the National Academy of Sciences*, **109**, **1215–20**. https://doi.org/10.1073/pnas.1117620109.

Berna, F., Matthews, A., Weiner, S. (2004). Solubilities of bone mineral from archaeological sites: The recrystallization window. *Journal of Archaeological Science*, **31**, **867–82**. https://doi.org/10.1016/j.jas.2003.12.003.

Bertrand, L., Vichi, A., Doucet, J., *et al.* (2014). The fate of archaeological keratin fibres in a temperate burial context: Microtaphonomy study of hairs from Marie de Bretagne (15th c., Orléans, France). *Journal of Archaeological Science*, **42**, **487–99**. https://doi.org/10.1016/j.jas.2013.11.028.

Birkenfeld, M., Avner, U., Bar-Yosef Mayer, D. E., *et al.* (2020). Hunting in the skies: Dating, paleoenvironment and archaeology at the late Pre-Pottery Neolithic B site of Nahal Roded 110, Eilat Mountains, Israel. *Paléorient*, **46(1–2)**, 43–68. https://doi.org/10.4000/paleorient.316.

Boaretto, E. (2008). Determining the chronology of an archaeological site using radiocarbon: Minimizing uncertainty. *Israel Journal of Earth Sciences*, **56**, **207–16**.

Boaretto, E. (2009). Dating materials in good archaeological contexts: The next challenge for radiocarbon analysis. *Radiocarbon*, **51(1)**, **275–81**. https://doi.org/10.1017/S0033822200033804.

Boaretto, E., Hernandez, M., Goder-Goldberger, M., *et al.* (2021). The absolute chronology of Boker Tachtit (Israel) and implications for the Middle to Upper

Paleolithic transition in the Levant. *Proceedings of the National Academy of Sciences*, **118(25)**, e2014657118. https://doi.org/10.1073/pnas.2014657118.

Boaretto, E., Poduska, K. M. (2013). Materials science challenges in radiocarbon dating: The case of archaeological plasters. *JOM*, **65**, 481–8. https://doi.org/10.1007/s11837-013-0573-8.

Boaretto, E., Wu, X., Yuan, J., *et al.* (2009). Radiocarbon dating of charcoal and bone collagen associated with early pottery at Yuchanyan Cave, Hunan Province, China. *Proceedings of the National Academy of Sciences*, **106 (24), 9595–9600**. https://doi.org/10.1073/pnas.0900539106.

Bowman, S. (1990). *Radiocarbon Dating*. London: University of California Press.

Boyatzis, S. C. (2022). Materials in Art and Archaeology through Their Infrared Spectra. Nova Science. https://doi.org/10.52305/SEYX8054.

Brown, K. S., Marean, C. W., Herries, A. I. R., *et al.* (2009). Fire as an engineering tool of early modern humans. *Science*, **325**, 859–62. https://doi.org/10.1126/science.1175028.

Burger, P., Stacey, R. J., Bowden, S. A., *et al.* (2016). Identification, geochemical characterisation and significance of bitumen among the grave goods of the 7th century mound 1 ship-burial at Sutton Hoo (Suffolk, UK). *PLoS ONE*, **11, e0166276**. https://doi.org/10.1371/journal.pone.0166276.

Burguet-Coca, A., Polo-Diáz, A., Martínez-Moreno, J., *et al.* (2020). Pen management and livestock activities based on phytoliths, dung spherulites, and minerals from Cova Gran de Santa Linya (Southeastern pre-Pyrenees). *Archaeological and Anthropological Sciences*, **12**, 148. https://doi.org/10.1007/s12520-020-01101-6.

Cabanes, D., Gadot, Y., Cabanes, M., *et al.* (2012). Human impact around settlement sites: A phytolith and mineralogical study for assessing site boundaries, phytolith preservation, and implications for spatial reconstructions using plant remains. *Journal of Archaeological Science*, **39**, 2697–707. https://doi.org/10.1016/j.jas.2012.04.008.

Cabanes, D., Mallol, C., Expósito, I., *et al.* (2010). Phytolith evidence for hearths and beds in the late Mousterian occupations of Esquilleu cave (Cantabria, Spain). *Journal of Archaeological Science*, **37**, 2947–57. https://doi.org/10.1016/j.jas.2010.07.010.

Cabanes, D., Weiner, S., Shahack-Gross, R. (2011). Stability of phytoliths in the archaeological record: A dissolution study of modern and fossil phytoliths. *Journal of Archaeological Science*, **38**, 2480–90. https://doi.org/10.1016/j.jas.2011.05.020.

Calandra, S., Cantisani, E., Salvadori, B., *et al.* (2022). Evaluation of ATR-FTIR spectroscopy for distinguishing anthropogenic and geogenic calcite. *Journal of Physics: Conference Series*, **2204**, **012048**. https://doi.org/ 10.1088/1742-6596/2204/1/012048.

Chowdhury, M. P., Choudhury, K. D., Potier Bouchard, G., *et al.* (2021). Machine learning ATR-FTIR spectroscopy data for the screening of collagen for ZooMS analysis and mtDNA in archaeological bone. *Journal of Archaeological Science*, **126**, **105311**. https://doi.org/10.1016/j.jas.2020.105311.

Chu, V., Regev, L., Weiner, S., *et al.* (2008). Differentiating between anthropogenic calcite in plaster, ash and natural calcite using infrared spectroscopy: Implications in archaeology. *Journal of Archaeological Science*, **35**, **905–11**. https://doi.org/10.1016/j.jas.2007.06.024.

Chukanov, N. V. (2014). *Infrared Spectra of Mineral Species*. Dordrecht: Springer. https://doi.org/10.1007/978-94-007-7128-4.

Cohen-Ofri, I., Weiner, L., Boaretto, E., *et al.* (2006). Modern and fossil charcoal: Aspects of structure and diagenesis. *Journal of Archaeological Science*, **33(3)**, **428–39**. https://doi.org/10.1016/j.jas.2005.08.008.

Cristiani, E., Lemorini, C., Saviola, D., *et al.* (2008). Anchor axes: A case-study of wear traces analysis on ethno-archaeological stone tools from Brazil. An anthropological reflection on functional meaning. In Longo, L., Skakun, N., eds., *"Prehistoric Technology" 40 Years Later: Functional Studies and the Russian Legacy*. Oxford: BAR, pp. **275–83**.

Dal Sasso, G., Asscher, A., Angelini, I., *et al.* (2018). A universal curve of apatite crystallinity for the assessment of bone integrity and preservation. *Scientific Reports*, **8**, **12025**. https://doi.org/10.1038/s41598-018-30642-z.

Dal Sasso, G., Lebon, M., Angelini, I., *et al.* (2016). Bone diagenesis variability among multiple burial phases at Al Khiday (Sudan) investigated by ATR-FTIR spectroscopy. *Palaeogeography, Palaeoclimatology, Palaeoecology*, **463**, **168–79**. https://doi.org/10.1016/j.palaeo.2016.10.005.

Dauphin, Y., Castillo-Michel, H., Denys, C., *et al.* (2018). Diagenetic alterations of *Meriones* incisors (Rodentia) of El Harhoura 2 cave, Morocco (late Pleistocene–middle Holocene). *Paläontologische Zeitschrift*, **92**, **163–77**. https://doi.org/10.1007/s12542-017-0382-4.

DeNiro, M. J., Weiner, S. (1988). Chemical, enzymatic and spectroscopic characterization of "collagen" and other organic fractions from prehistoric bones. *Geochimica et Cosmochimica Acta*, **52**, **2197–206**. https://doi.org/ 10.1016/0016-7037(88)90122-6.

Derrick, M. R., Stulik, D., Landry, J. M. (1999). *Infrared Spectroscopy in Conservation Science*. Los Angeles: The Getty Conservation Institute. www.getty.edu/publications/virtuallibrary/0892364696.html.

Diem, M. (2015). *Modern Vibrational Spectroscopy and Micro-Spectroscopy*. Chichester: John Wiley. https://doi.org/10.1002/9781118824924.

Domingo, I., García-Borja, P., Roldán, C. (2012). Identification, processing and use of red pigments (hematite and cinnabar) in the Valencian Early Neolithic (Spain). *Archaeometry*, **54(5)**, **868**–**92**. https://doi.org/10.1111/j.1475-4754.2011.00650.x.

Dunseth, Z. C., Shahack-Gross, R. (2018). Calcitic dung spherulites and the potential for rapid identification of degraded animal dung at archaeological sites using FTIR spectroscopy. *Journal of Archaeological Science*, **97**, **118**–**24**. https://doi.org/10.1016/j.jas.2018.07.005.

Duyckaerts, G. (1959). The infra-red analysis of solid substances: A review. *Analyst*, **84(997)**, **201**–**14**. https://doi.org/10.1039/AN9598400201.

Eliyahu-Behar, A., Shai, I., Gur-Arieh, S., *et al.* (2017a). Early Bronze Age pebble installations from Tell es-Safi/Gath, Israel: Evidence for their function and utilization. *Levant*, **49**, **46**–**63**. https://doi.org/10.1080/00758914.2017.1279495.

Eliyahu-Behar, A., Shilstein, S., Raban-Gerstel, N., *et al.* (2008). An integrated approach to reconstructing primary activities from pit deposits: Iron smithing and other activities at Tel Dor under Neo-Assyrian domination. *Journal of Archaeological Science*, **35**, **2895**–**908**. https://doi.org/10.1016/j.jas.2008.06.004.

Eliyahu-Behar, A., Yahalom-Mack, N., Ben-Shlomo, D. (2017). Excavation and analysis of an early Iron Age lime kiln. *Israel Exploration Journal*, **67**, **14**–**31**. www.jstor.org/stable/44474015.

Eliyahu-Behar, A., Yahalom-Mack, N., Shilstein, S., *et al.* (2012). Iron and bronze production in Iron Age IIA Philistia: New evidence from Tell es-Safi/ Gath, Israel. *Journal of Archaeological Science*, **39**, **255**–**67**. https://doi.org/10.1016/j.jas.2011.09.002.

Esteban, I., Fitchett, J. M., de la Peña, P. (2020). Plant taphonomy, flora exploitation and palaeoenvironments at the Middle Stone Age site of Mwulu's Cave (Limpopo, South Africa): An archaeobotanical and mineralogical approach. *Archaeological and Anthropological Sciences*, **12**, **226**. https://doi.org/10.1007/s12520-020-01181-4.

Esteban, I., Marean, C. W., Fisher, E. C., *et al.* (2018). Phytoliths as an indicator of early modern humans plant gathering strategies, fire fuel and site occupation intensity during the Middle Stone Age at Pinnacle Point 5-6 (south coast, South Africa). *PLoS ONE*, **13(6)**, **e0198558**. https://doi.org/10.1371/journal.pone.0198558.

Fahrenfort, J. (1961). Attenuated total reflection: A new principle for the production of useful infrared reflection spectra of organic compounds. *Spectrochimica Acta*, **17(7)**, **698**–**709**. https://doi.org/10.1016/0371-1951(61)80136-7.

Farmer, V. C. (ed.) (1974). *The Infrared Spectra of Minerals*. London: Mineralogical Society. https://doi.org/10.1180/mono-4.

Featherstone, J. D. B., Pearson, S., LeGeros, R. Z. (1984). An infrared method for quantification of carbonate in carbonated apatites. *Caries Research*, **18**, 63–6. https://doi.org/10.1159/000260749.

Fernández-Palacios, E., Jambrina-Enríquez, M., Mentzer, S. M., *et al.* (2023). Reconstructing formation processes at the Canary Islands indigenous site of Belmaco Cave (La Palma, Spain) through a multiproxy geoarchaeological approach. *Geoarchaeology: An International Journal*, **38(6)**, 713–39. https://doi.org/10.1002/gea.21972.

Finkelstein, I., Ben Dor Evian, S., Boaretto, E., *et al.* (2012). Reconstructing ancient Israel: Integrating macro- and micro-archaeology. *Hebrew Bible and Ancient Israel*, **1(1)**, 133–50. https://doi.org/10.1628/219222712801608531.

Forget, M., Regev, L., Friesem, D. E., *et al.* (2015). Physical and mineralogical properties of experimentally heated chaff-tempered mud bricks: Implications for reconstruction of environmental factors influencing the appearance of mud bricks in archaeological conflagration events. *Journal of Archaeological Science: Reports*, **2**, 80–93. https://doi.org/10.1016/j.jasrep.2015.01.008.

Freeman, C. L., Dieudonné, L., Agbaje, O. B. A., *et al.* (2023). Survival of environmental DNA in sediments: Mineralogic control on DNA taphonomy. *Environmental DNA*, **5(6)**, 1691–705. https://doi.org/10.1002/edn3.482.

Friesem, D. E., Abadi, I., Shaham, D., *et al.* (2019). Lime plaster cover of the dead 12,000 years ago – new evidence for the origins of lime plaster technology. *Evolutionary Human Sciences*, **1**, e9. https://doi.org/10.1017/ehs.2019.9.

Friesem, D. E., Shahack-Gross, R., Weinstein-Evron, M., *et al.* (2021a). High-resolution study of Middle Palaeolithic deposits and formation processes at Tabun Cave, Israel: Guano-rich cave deposits and detailed stratigraphic appreciation of Layer C. *Quaternary Science Reviews*, **274**, 107203. https://doi.org/10.1016/j.quascirev.2021.107203.

Friesem, D. E., Teutsch, N., Weinstein-Evron, M., *et al.* (2021b). Identification of fresh and burnt bat guano and pigeon droppings in Eastern Mediterranean karstic cave sites based on micromorphological and chemical characteristics. *Quaternary Science Reviews*, **274**, 107238. https://doi.org/10.1016/j.quascirev.2021.107238.

Friesem, D. E., Zaidner, Y., Shahack-Gross, R. (2014). Formation processes and combustion features at the lower layers of the Middle Palaeolithic open-air site of Nesher Ramla, Israel. *Quaternary International*, **331**, 128–38. https://doi.org/10.1016/j.quaint.2013.03.023.

Gaffney, J. S., Marley, N. A., Jones, D. E. (2012). Fourier Transform Infrared (FTIR) spectroscopy. In Kaufmann, E. N., ed., *Characterization of Materials*. John Wiley. https://doi.org/10.1002/0471266965.com107.pub2.

Gallo, G., Ushakov, S. V., Navrotsky, A., Stahlschmidt, M. C. (2023). Impact of prolonged heating on the color and crystallinity of bone. *Archaeological and Anthropological Sciences*, **15**, **143**. https://doi.org/10.1007/s12520-023-01842-0.

Geiger, S. B., Weiner, S. (1993). Fluoridated carbonatoapatite in the intermediate layer between glass ionomer and dentin. *Dental Materials*, **9(1)**, **33–6**. https://doi.org/10.1016/0109-5641(93)90102-V.

Goldberg, P., Berna, F. (2010). Micromorphology and context. *Quaternary International*, **214(1–2)**, **56–62**. https://doi.org/10.1016/j.quaint.2009.10.023.

Goldberg, P., Miller, C. E., Mentzer, S. M. (2017). Recognizing fire in the Paleolithic Archaeological record. *Current Anthropology*, **58(16)**, **175–90**. https://doi.org/10.1086/692729.

Goshen, N., Yasur-Landau, A., Cline, E. H., *et al.* (2017). Palatial architecture under the microscope: Production, maintenance, and spatiotemporal changes gleaned from plastered surfaces at a Canaanite palace complex, Tel Kabri, Israel. *Journal of Archaeological Science: Reports*, **11**, **189–99**. https://doi.org/10.1016/j.jasrep.2016.11.039.

Grono, E., Piper, P. J., Kinh, D. N., *et al.* (2022). Early settlement construction in Southeast Asia: Lime mortar floor sequences at Loc Giang, southern Vietnam. *Antiquity*, **96(390)**, **1538–54**. https://doi.org/10.15184/aqy.2022.139.

Grün, R. Schwarcz, H. P., Chadam, J. (1988). ESR dating of tooth enamel: Coupled correction for U-uptake and U-series disequilibrium. *International Journal of Radiation Applications and Instrumentation. Part D. Nuclear Tracks and Radiation Measurements*, **14(1–2)**, **237–41**. https://doi.org/10.1016/1359-0189(88)90071-4.

Gueta, R., Natan, A., Addadi, L., *et al.* (2006). Local atomic order and infrared spectra of biogenic calcite. *Angewandte Chemie*, **46(1–2)**, **291–4**. https://doi.org/10.1002/anie.200603327.

Guiliano, M., Asia, L., Onoratini, G., *et al.* (2007). Applications of diamond crystal ATR FTIR spectroscopy to the characterization of ambers. *Spectrochimica Acta Part A*, **67**, **1407–11**. https://doi.org/10.1016/j.saa.2006.10.033.

Herschel, W. (1800). Experiments on the Refrangibility of the invisible Rays of the Sun. *Philosophical Transactions of the Royal Society of London*, **90**, **284–92**. https://doi.org/10.1098/rstl.1800.0015.

Herzberg, G. (1945). *Infrared and Raman Spectra of Polyatomic Molecules*. New York: D. Van Nostrand. https://archive.org/details/in.ernet.dli.2015.177114/page/n1/mode/2up.

Humecki, H. J. (ed.) (1995). *Practical Guide to Infrared Microspectroscopy.* New York: Marcel Dekker.

Karkanas, P. (2021). All about wood ash: Long term fire experiments reveal unknown aspects of the formation and preservation of ash with critical implications on the emergence and use of fire in the past. *Journal of Archaeological Science*, **135**, **105476**. https://doi.org/10.1016/j.jas.2021.105476.

Karkanas, P., Bar-Yosef, O., Goldberg, P., *et al.* (2000). Diagenesis in prehistoric caves: The use of minerals that form *in situ* to assess the completeness of the archaeological record. *Journal of Archaeological Science*, **27**, **915–29**. https://doi.org/10.1006/jasc.1999.0506.

Karkanas, P., Berna, F., Fallu, D., *et al.* (2019). Microstratigraphic and mineralogical study of a Late Bronze Age updraft pottery kiln, Kolonna site, Aegina Island, Greece. *Archaeological and Anthropological Sciences*, **11**, **5763–80**. https://doi.org/10.1007/s12520-019-00903-7.

Karkanas, P., Goldberg, P. (2019). *Reconstructing Archaeological Sites: Understanding the Geoarchaeological Matrix.* Chichester: John Wiley. https://doi.org/10.1002/9781119016427.

Karkanas, P., Koumouzelis, M., Kozlowski, J. K., *et al.* (2004). The earliest evidence for clay hearths: Aurignacian features in Klisoura Cave 1, southern Greece. *Antiquity*, **78(301)**, **513–25**. https://doi.org/10.1017/S0003598X00113195.

Karkanas, P., Kyparissi-Apostolika, N., Bar-Yosef, O., *et al.* (1999). Mineral assemblages in Theopetra, Greece: A framework for understanding diagenesis in a prehistoric cave. *Journal of Archaeological Science*, **26(9)**, **1171–80**. https://doi.org/10.1006/jasc.1998.0354.

Karkanas, P., Rigaud, J.-P., Simek, J. F., *et al.* (2002). Ash bones and guano: A study of the minerals and phytoliths in the sediments of Grotte XVI, Dordogne, France. *Journal of Archaeological Science*, **29(7)**, **721–32**. https://doi.org/10.1006/jasc.2001.0742.

Karkanas, P., Shahack-Gross, R., Ayalon, A., *et al.* (2007). Evidence for habitual use of fire at the end of the Lower Paleolithic: Site-formation processes at Qesem Cave, Israel. *Journal of Human Evolution*, **53**, **197–212**. https://doi.org/10.1016/j.jhevol.2007.04.002.

Kaur, H, Rana, B., Tomar, D., *et al.* (2021). Fundamentals of ATR-FTIR spectroscopy and its role for probing in-situ molecular-level interactions. In Singh, D. K., Pradhan, M., Materny, A., eds., *Modern Techniques of Spectroscopy.* Springer, pp. **3–37**. https://doi.org/10.1007/978-981-33-6084-6_1.

Kingery, W. D., Vandiver, P. B., Prickett, M. (1988). The Beginnings of pyrotechnology, Part II: Production and use of lime and gypsum plaster in the Pre-Pottery Neolithic Near East. *Journal of Field Archaeology*, **15(2)**, 219–44. https://Doi.org/10.1179/009346988791974501.

Kirkbride, K. P. (2009). Microscopy: FTIR. In Jamieson, A., Moenssens, A., eds., *Wiley Encyclopedia of Forensic Science*. John Wiley. https://doi.org/10.1002/9780470061589.fsa084.

Larbey, C., Mentzer, S. M., Ligouis, B., *et al.* (2019). Cooked starchy food in hearths ca. 120 kya and 65 kya (MIS 5e and MIS 4) from Klasies River Cave, South Africa. *Journal of Human Evolution*, **131**, 210–27. https://doi.org/10.1016/j.jhevol.2019.03.015.

Lebon, M., Müller, K., Bahain, J.-J., *et al.* (2011). Imaging fossil bone alterations at the microscale by SR-FTIR microspectroscopy. *Journal of Analytical Atomic Spectrometry*, **26**, 922–29. https://doi.org/10.1039/C0JA00250J.

Lebon, M., Reiche, I., Bahain, J.-J., *et al.* (2010). New parameters for the characterization of diagenetic alterations and heat-induced changes of fossil bone mineral using Fourier transform infrared spectrometry. *Journal of Archaeological Science*, **37(9)**, 2265–76. https://doi.org/10.1016/j.jas.2010.03.024.

Lebon, M., Reiche, I., Gallet, X., *et al.* (2016). Rapid quantification of bone collagen content by ATR-FTIR spectroscopy. *Radiocarbon*, **58(1)**, 131–45. https://doi.org/10.1017/RDC.2015.11.

Lebon, M., Zazzo, A., Reiche, I., (2014). Screening in situ bone and teeth preservation by ATR-FTIR mapping. *Palaeogeography, Palaeoclimatology, Palaeoecology*, **416**, 110–9. https://doi.org/10.1016/j.palaeo.2014.08.001.

LeGeros, R. Z. (1991). *Calcium Phosphates in Oral Biology and Medicine*. Basel: Karger.

Lin-Vien, D., Colthup, N. B., Fateley, W. G., *et al.* (1991), *The Handbook of Infrared and Raman Characteristic Frequencies of Organic Molecules*. San Diego: Academic Press. https://doi.org/10.1016/B978-0-08-057116-4.50001-8.

Loftus, E., Rogers, K., Lee-Thorp, J. (2015). A simple method to establish calcite:aragonite ratios in archaeological mollusc shells. *Journal of Quaternary Science*, **30(8)**, 731–5. https://doi.org/10.1002/jqs.2819.

Madejová, J. (2003). FTIR techniques in clay mineral studies. *Vibrational Spectroscopy*, **31**, 1–10. https://doi.org/10.1016/S0924-2031(02)00065-6.

Mallol, C., Cabanes, D., Baena, J. (2010). Microstratigraphy and diagenesis at the upper Pleistocene site of Esquilleu Cave (Cantabria, Spain). *Quaternary International*, **214**, 70–81. https://doi.org/10.1016/j.quaint.2009.10.018.

Mamede, A. P., Gonçalves, D., Marques, M. P. M., *et al.* (2018). Burned bones tell their own stories: A review of methodological approaches to assess heat-induced diagenesis. *Applied Spectroscopy Reviews*, **53(8)**, **603–35**. https://Doi.org/10.1080/05704928.2017.1400442.

Maor, Y., Toffolo, M. B., Feldman, Y., *et al.* (2023). Dolomite in archaeological plaster: An FTIR study of the plaster floors at Neolithic Motza, Israel. *Journal of Archaeological Science: Reports*, **48**, **103862**. https://doi.org/10.1016/j.jasrep.2023.103862.

Margaris, A. V. (2014). Fourier Transform Infrared Spectroscopy (FTIR): Applications in archaeology. In Smith, C., ed., *Encyclopedia of Global Archaeology*. New York: Springer, pp. **2890-3**. https://doi.org/10.1007/978-1-4419-0465-2_343.

Massilani, D., Morley, M. W., Mentzer, S. M., *et al.* (2022). Microstratigraphic preservation of ancient faunal and hominin DNA in Pleistocene cave sediments. *Proceedings of the National Academy of Sciences*, **119(1)**, **e2113666118**. https://doi.org/10.1073/pnas.2113666118.

Mentzer, S. M. (2014). Microarchaeological approaches to the identification and interpretation of combustion features in prehistoric archaeological sites. *Journal of Archaeological Method and Theory*, **21**, **616–68**. https://doi.org/10.1007/s10816-012-9163-2.

Mercier, N., Valladas, H., Froget, L., *et al.* (2007). Hayonim Cave: a TL-based chronology for this Levantine Mousterian sequence. *Journal of Archaeological Science*, **34(7)**, **1064–77**. https://doi.org/10.1016/j.jas.2006.09.021.

Mercier, N., Valladas, H., Joron, J. L., *et al.* (1995). Thermoluminescence dating and the problem of geochemical evolution of sediments – A case study: The Mousterian levels at Hayonim. *Israel Journal of Chemistry*, **35(2)**, **13741**. https://doi.org/10.1002/ijch.199500021.

Messerschmidt, R. G., Harthcock, M. A. (eds.) (1988). *Infrared Microspectroscopy: Theory and Applications*. New York: Marcel Dekker.

Miller, L. M., Dumas, P. (2006). Chemical imaging of biological tissue with synchrotron infrared light. *Biochimica et Biophysica Acta (BBA) – Biomembranes*, **1758(7)**, **846–57**. https://doi.org/10.1016/j.bbamem.2006.04.010.

Monnier, G. F. (2018). A review of infrared spectroscopy in microarchaeology: Methods, applications, and recent trends. *Journal of Archaeological Science: Reports*, **18**, **806–23**. https://doi.org/10.1016/j.jasrep.2017.12.029.

Mourre, V., Villa, P., Henshilwood, C. S. (2010). Early use of pressure flaking on lithic artifacts at Blombos Cave, South Africa. *Science*, **330**, **659–62**. https://doi.org/10.1126/science.1195550.

Namdar, D., Zukerman, A., Maeir, A. M., *et al.* (2011). The 9th century BCE destruction layer at Tell es-Safi/Gath, Israel: Integrating macro- and microarchaeology. *Journal of Archaeological Science*, **38**, 3471–82. https://doi.org/10.1016/j.jas.2011.08.009.

Newesely, H. (1989). Fossil bone apatite. *Applied Geochemistry*, **4**, 233–45. https://doi.org/10.1016/0883-2927(89)90023-1.

Ogloblin Ramírez, I., Dunseth, Z. C., Shalem, D., *et al.* (2023). Infrared spectra of mixtures of heated and unheated clay: Solving an interpretational conundrum. *Geoarchaeology: An International Journal*, **38(6)**, 822–9. https://doi.org/10.1002/gea.21976.

Ortiz Ruiz, S., de Lucio, O. G., Mitrani Viggiano, A., *et al.* (2023). Mayan fire: Calibration curve for the determination of heating temperatures of limestone, lime and related materials by FTIR measurements. *Journal of Archaeological Science: Reports*, **49**, 103966. https://doi.org/10.1016/j.jasrep.2023.103966.

Oskam, C. L., Haile, J., McLay, E., *et al.* (2010). Fossil avian eggshell preserves ancient DNA. *Proceedings of the Royal Society B*, **277**, 1991–2000. https://doi.org/10.1098/rspb.2009.2019.

Patania, I., Goldberg, P., Cohen, D. J., *et al.* (2019). Micromorphological and FTIR analysis of the Upper Paleolithic early pottery site of Yuchanyan cave, Hunan, South China. *Geoarchaeology: An International Journal*, **35(2)**, 143–63. https://doi.org/10.1002/gea.21771.

Piga, G., Santos-Cubedo, A., Brunetti, A., *et al.* (2011). A multi-technique approach by XRD, XRF, FT-IR to characterize the diagenesis of dinosaur bones from Spain. *Palaeogeography, Palaeoclimatology, Palaeoecology*, **310**, 92–107. https://doi.org/10.1016/j.palaeo.2011.05.018.

Poduska, K. M., Regev, L., Berna, F., *et al.* (2012). Plaster characterization at the PPNB site of Yiftahel (Israel) including the use of [14]C: Implications for plaster production, preservation, and dating. *Radiocarbon*, **54(3–4)**, 887–96. https://doi.org/10.1017/S0033822200047536.

Poduska, K. M., Regev, L., Boaretto, E., *et al.* (2011). Decoupling local disorder and optical effects in infrared spectra: Differentiating between calcites with different origins. *Advanced Materials*, **23**, 550–4. https://doi.org/10.1002/adma.201003890.

Pons-Branchu, E. (2023). U-Series dating in archaeology. In Pollard, M. A., Armitage, R. A., Makarewicz, C. A., eds., *Handbook of Archaeological Sciences*. Chichester: John Wiley, pp. 89–97. https://doi.org/10.1002/9781119592112.ch5.

Pons-Branchu, E., Barbarand, J., Caffy, I., *et al.* (2022). U-series and radiocarbon cross dating of speleothems from Nerja Cave (Spain): Evidence of open system behavior. Implication for the Spanish rock art chronology. *Quaternary Science Reviews*, **290**, 107634. https://doi.org/10.1016/j.quascirev.2022.107634.

Pothier Bouchard, G., Mentzer, S. M., Riel-Salvatore, J., *et al.* (2019). Portable FTIR for on-site screening of archaeological bone intended for ZooMS collagen fingerprint analysis. *Journal of Archaeological Science: Reports*, **26**, **101862**. https://doi.org/10.1016/j.jasrep.2019.05.027.

Rebollo, N. R., Cohen-Ofri, I., Popovitz-Biro, R., *et al.* (2008). Structural characterization of charcoal exposed to high and low pH: Implications for ^{14}C sample preparation and charcoal preservation. *Radiocarbon*, **50(2)**, **289–307**. https://doi.org/10.1017/S0033822200033592.

Rebollo, N. R., Weiner, S., Brock, F., *et al.* (2011). New radiocarbon dating of the transition from the Middle to the Upper Paleolithic in Kebara Cave, Israel. *Journal of Archaeological Science*, **38(9)**, **2424–33**. https://doi.org/10.1016/j.jas.2011.05.010.

Regert, M., Colinart, S., Degrand, L., *et al.* (2001). Chemical alteration and use of beeswax through time: Accelerated ageing tests and analysis of archaeological samples from various environmental contexts. *Archaeometry*, **43(4)**, **549–69**. https://doi.org/10.1111/1475-4754.00036.

Regev, L., Cabanes, D., Homsher, R., *et al.* (2015). Geoarchaeological investigation in a domestic Iron Age Quarter, Tel Megiddo, Israel. *Bulletin of the American Schools of Oriental Research*, **374**, **135–57**. https://doi.org/10.5615/bullamerschoorie.374.0135.

Regev, L., Eckmeier, E., Mintz, E., *et al.* (2011). Radiocarbon concentrations of wood ash calcite: Potential for dating. *Radiocarbon*, **53(1)**, **117–27**. https://doi.org/10.1017/S0033822200034391.

Regev, L., Poduska, K. M., Addadi, L., *et al.* (2010a). Distinguishing between calcites formed by different mechanisms using infrared spectrometry: Archaeological applications. *Journal of Archaeological Science*, **37(12)**, **3022–9**. https://doi.org/10.1016/j.jas.2010.06.027.

Regev, L., Zukerman, A., Hitchcock, L., *et al.* (2010b). Iron Age hydraulic plaster from Tell es-Safi/Gath, Israel. *Journal of Archaeological Science*, **37 (12)**, **3000–9**. https://doi.org/10.1016/j.jas.2010.06.023.

Reidsma, F. H. (2022). Laboratory-based experimental research into the effect of diagenesis on heated bone: Implications and improved tools for the characterisation of ancient fire. *Scientific Reports*, **12**, **17544**. https://doi.org/10.1038/s41598-022-21622-5.

Reidsma, F. H., van Hoesel, A., van Os, B. J. H., *et al.* (2016). Charred bone: Physical and chemical changes during laboratory simulated heating under reducing conditions and its relevance for the study of fire use in archaeology. *Journal of Archaeological Science: Reports*, **10**, **282–92**. https://doi.org/10.1016/j.jasrep.2016.10.001.

Rhodes, S. E., Goldberg, P., Ecker, M., *et al.* (2022). Exploring the Later Stone Age at a micro-scale: New high-resolution excavations at Wonderwerk Cave. *Quaternary International*, **614**, **126**–45. https://doi.org/10.1016/j.quaint.2021.10.004.

Richard, M. (2023). Trapped charge dating and archaeology. In Pollard, M. A., Armitage, R. A., Makarewicz, C. A., eds., *Handbook of Archaeological Sciences*. Chichester: John Wiley, pp. **69**–87. https://doi.org/10.1002/9781119592112.ch4.

Richard, M., Kaplan-Ashiri, I., Alonso, M. J., *et al.* (2023). New ESR dates from Lovedale, Free State, South Africa: Implications for the study of tooth diagenesis. *South African Archaeological Bulletin*, **78(219)**, **95**–103. https://cnrs.hal.science/hal-04378183/file/RICHARD%20et%20al._2023_SAAB.pdf.

Richard, M., Pons-Branchu, E., Carmieli, R., *et al.* (2022). Investigating the effect of diagenesis on ESR dating of Middle Stone Age tooth samples from the open-air site of Lovedale, Free State, South Africa. *Quaternary Geochronology*, **69**, **101269**. https://doi.org/10.1016/j.quageo.2022.101269.

Rink, W. J., Schwarcz, H. P., Weiner, S., *et al.* (2004). Age of the Mousterian industry at Hayonim Cave, Northern Israel, using electron spin resonance and ^{230}Th/^{234}U methods. *Journal of Archaeological Science*, **31(7)**, **953**–64. https://doi.org/10.1016/j.jas.2003.12.009.

Rubens, H., Nichols, E. F. (1897). Versuche mit Wärmerstrahlen von grosser Wellenlänge. *Annalen der Physik*, **296(3)**, **418**–62. https://doi.org/10.1002/andp.18972960303.

Sandgathe, D. M., Berna, F. (2017). Fire and the genus *Homo*. *Current Anthropology*, **58(16)**, **165**–74. https://doi.org/10.1086/691424.

Schiegl, S., Goldberg, P., Bar-Yosef, O., *et al.* (1996). Ash deposits in Hayonim and Kebara caves, Israel: Macroscopic, microscopic and mineralogical observations, and their archaeological implications. *Journal of Archaeological Science*, **23**, **763**–81. https://doi.org/10.1006/jasc.1996.0071.

Schiegl, S., Goldberg, P., Pfretzschner, H.-U., *et al.* (2003). Paleolithic burnt bone horizons from the Swabian Jura: Distinguishing between *in situ* fireplaces and dumping areas. *Geoarchaeology: An International Journal*, **18(5)**, **541**–65. https://doi.org/10.1002/gea.10080.

Schiegl, S., Lev-Yadun, S., Bar-Yosef, O., *et al.* (1994). Siliceous aggregates from prehistoric wood ash: A major component of sediments in Kebara and Hayonim caves (Israel). *Israel Journal of Earth Sciences*, **43**, **267**–78.

Schmidt, P., Frölich, F. (2011). Temperature dependent crystallographic transformations in chalcedony, SiO_2, assessed in mid infrared spectroscopy.

Spectrochimica Acta Part A: Molecular and Biomolecular Spectroscopy, **78 (5)**, **1476–81**. https://doi.org/10.1016/j.saa.2011.01.036.

Schmidt, P., Badou, A., Frölich, F. (2011). Detailed FT near-infrared study of the behaviour of water and hydroxyl in sedimentary length-fast chalcedony, SiO_2, upon heat treatment. *Spectrochimica Acta Part A: Molecular and Biomolecular Spectroscopy*, **81**, **552–9**. https://doi.org/10.1016/j.saa.2011.06.050.

Schmidt, P., Bellot-Gurlet, L., Léa, V., *et al.* (2013a). Moganite detection in silica rocks using Raman and infrared spectroscopy. *European Journal of Mineralogy*, **25(5)**, **797–805**. https://doi.org/10.1127/0935-1221/2013/0025-2274.

Schmidt, P., Koch, T., Blessing, M. A., *et al.* (2023). Production method of the Königsaue birch tar documents cumulative culture in Neanderthals. *Archaeological and Anthropological Sciences*, **15**, **84**. https://doi.org/10.1007/s12520-023-01789-2.

Schmidt, P., Masse, S., Laurent, G., *et al.* (2012). Crystallographic and structural transformations of sedimentary chalcedony in flint upon heat treatment. *Journal of Archaeological Science*, **39**, **135–44**. https://doi.org/10.1016/j.jas.2011.09.012.

Schmidt, P., Porraz, G., Slodczyk, A., *et al.* (2013b). Heat treatment in the South African Middle Stone Age: Temperature induced transformations of silcrete and their technological implications. *Journal of Archaeological Science*, **40**, **3519–31**. https://doi.org/10.1016/j.jas.2012.10.016.

Schmidt, P., Stynder, D., Conard, N. J., *et al.* (2020). When was silcrete heat treatment invented in South Africa? *Palgrave Communications*, **6**, **73**. https://doi.org/10.1057/s41599-020-0454-z.

Schrader, B. (ed.) (1995). *Infrared and Raman Spectroscopy*. New York: VCH. https://doi.org/10.1002/9783527615438.

Shahack-Gross, R., Berna, F., Karkanas, P., *et al.* (2004a). Bat guano and preservation of archaeological remains in cave sites. *Journal of Archaeological Science*, **31**, **1259–72**. https://doi.org/10.1016/j.jas.2004.02.004.

Shahack-Gross, R., Berna, F., Karkanas, P., *et al.* (2014). Evidence for the repeated use of a central hearth at Middle Pleistocene (300 ky ago) Qesem Cave, Israel. *Journal of Archaeological Science*, **44**, **12–21**. https://doi.org/10.1016/j.jas.2013.11.015.

Shahack-Gross, R., Marshall, F., Ryan, K., *et al.* (2004b). Reconstruction of spatial organization in abandoned Maasai settlements: Implications for site structure in the Pastoral Neolithic of East Africa. *Journal of Archaeological Science*, **31**, **1395–411**. https://doi.org/10.1016/j.jas.2004.03.003.

Shahack-Gross, R., Marshall, F., Weiner, S. (2003). Geo-Ethnoarchaeology of pastoral sites: The identification of livestock enclosures in abandoned Maasai settlements. *Journal of Archaeological Science*, **30**, 439–59. https://doi.org/10.1006/jasc.2002.0853.

Shalom, N., Vaknin, Y., Shaar, R., *et al.* (2023). Destruction by fire: Reconstructing the evidence of the 586 BCE Babylonian destruction in a monumental building in Jerusalem. *Journal of Archaeological Science*, **157**, 105823. https://doi.org/10.1016/j.jas.2023.105823.

Shaw, C. L. (2022). An evaluation of the infrared 630 cm^{-1} OH libration band in bone mineral as evidence of fire in the archaeological record. *Journal of Archaeological Science: Reports*, **46**, **103655**. https://doi.org/10.1016/j.jasrep.2022.103655.

Shipman, P., Foster, G., Schoeninger, M. (1984). Burnt bones and teeth: An experimental study of color, morphology, crystal structure and shrinkage. *Journal of Archaeological Science*, **11**, **307–25**. https://doi.org/10.1016/0305-4403(84)90013-X.

Shoval, S. (1993). Burning temperature of a Persian-period pottery kiln at Tel Michal, Israel, estimated from the composition of slag-like material formed in its wall. *Journal of Thermal Analysis*, **39(8–9)**, **1157–68**.

Shoval, S. (1994). The firing temperature of a Persian-period pottery kiln at Tel Michal, Israel, estimated from the composition of its pottery. *Journal of Thermal Analysis*, 42(1), **175–85**. https://doi.org/10.1007/bf02546999.

Shoval, S. (2017). Fourier Transform Infrared Spectroscopy (FT-IR) in Archaeological Ceramic Analysis. In Hunt, A., ed., *The Oxford Handbook of Archaeological Ceramic Analysis*. Oxford: Oxford University Press, pp. **509–30**. https://doi.org/10.1093/oxfordhb/9780199681532.013.28.

Shoval, S., Ginott, Y., Nathan, Y. (1991). A new method for measuring the crystallinity index of quartz by infrared spectroscopy. *Mineralogical Magazine*, **55**, **579–82**. https://doi.org/10.1180/minmag.1991.055.381.10.

Simões, C. D., Aldeias, V. (2022). Thermo-microstratigraphy of shells reveals invisible fire use and possible cooking in the archaeological record. *Frontiers in Earth Science*, **10**, 869487. https://doi.org/10.3389/feart.2022.869487.

Sponheimer, M., Lee-Thorp, J. A. (1999). Alteration of enamel carbonate environments during fossilization. *Journal of Archaeological Science*, **26**, **143–50**. https://doi.org/10.1006/jasc.1998.0293.

Stahlschmidt, M. C., Miller, C. E., Ligouis, B., *et al.* (2015). On the evidence for human use and control of fire at Schöningen. *Journal of Human Evolution*, **89**, **181–201**. https://doi.org/10.1016/j.jhevol.2015.04.004.

Stepka, Z., Azuri, I., Horwitz, L. K., *et al.* (2022). Hidden signatures of early fire at Evron Quarry (1.0 to 0.8 Mya). *Proceedings of the National Academy of Sciences*, **119(25)**, e2123439119. https://doi.org/10.1073/pnas.2123439119.

Stevenson, C. M., Ladefoged, T. N., Novak, S. W. (2013). Prehistoric settlement chronology on Rapa Nui, Chile: Obsidian hydration dating using infrared photoacoustic spectroscopy. *Journal of Archaeological Science*, **40**, **3021–30**. https://doi.org/10.1016/j.jas.2013.03.019.

Stewart, B. A., Zhao, Y., Mitchell, P. J., *et al.* (2020). Ostrich eggshell bead strontium isotopes reveal persistent macroscale social networking across late quaternary southern Africa. *Proceedings of the National Academy of Sciences*, **117(12)**, **6453–62**. https://doi.org/10.1073/pnas.1921037117.

Stimson, M. M., O'Donnell, M. J. (1952). The infrared and ultraviolet spectra of cystine and isocystine in the solid state. *Journal of the American Chemical Society*, **74**, **1805–8**. https://doi.org/10.1021/ja01127a054.

Stiner, M. C., Kuhn, S. L., Surovell, T. A., *et al.* (2001). Bone preservation in Hayonim Cave (Israel): A macroscopic and mineralogical study. *Journal of Archaeological Science*, **28(6)**, **643–59**. https://doi.org/10.1006/jasc.2000.0634.

Stiner, M. C., Kuhn, S. L., Weiner, S., *et al.* (1995). Differential burning, recrystallization, and fragmentation of archaeological bone. *Journal of Archaeological Science*, **22**, **223–37**. https://doi.org/10.1006/jasc.1995.0024.

Suzuki, M., Dauphin, Y., Addadi, L., *et al.* (2011). Atomic order of aragonite crystals formed by mollusks. *CrystEngComm*, **13**, **6780–6**. https://doi.org/10.1039/C1CE05572K.

Tang, Y., Gao, J., Liu, C., *et al.* (2019). Dehydration pathways of Gypsum and the rehydration mechanism of soluble anhydrite γ-$CaSO_4$. *ACS Omega*, **4**, **7636–42**. https://doi.org/10.1021/acsomega.8b03476.

Termine, J. D., Posner, A. S. (1966). Infrared analysis of rat bone: Age dependency of amorphous and crystalline mineral fractions. *Science*, **153**, **1523–25**. https://doi.org/10.1126/science.153.3743.1523.

Thibodeau, M. L. (2016). Identifying 1 mya fire in Wonderwerk Cave with micromorphology and Fourier Transform infrared microspectroscopy. Unpublished M. A. thesis, Department of Archaeology, Simon Fraser University. https://summit.sfu.ca/item/16644.

Thompson, T. J. U., Islam, M., Bonniere, M. (2013). A new statistical approach for determining the crystallinity of heat-altered bone mineral from FTIR spectra. *Journal of Archaeological Science*, **40**, **416–22**. https://doi.org/10.1016/j.jas.2012.07.008.

Toffolo, M. B. (2018). Microarchaeology. In López Varela, S. L., ed., *The Encyclopedia of Archaeological Sciences*. John Wiley. https://doi.org/10.1002/9781119188230.saseas0377.

Toffolo, M. B. (2020). Radiocarbon dating of anthropogenic carbonates: What is the benchmark for sample selection? *Heritage*, **3(4)**, **1416–32**. https://doi.org/10.3390/heritage3040079.

Toffolo, M. B. (2021). The significance of aragonite in the interpretation of the microscopic archaeological record. *Geoarchaeology: An International Journal*, **36**, 149–69. https://doi.org/10.1002/gea.21816.

Toffolo, M. B., Berna, F. (2018). Infrared absorption spectroscopy (IR, FTIR, DRIFT, ATR). In López Varela, S. L., ed., *The Encyclopedia of Archaeological Sciences*. John Wiley. https://doi.org/10.1002/9781119188230.saseas0325.

Toffolo M. B., Boaretto, E. (2014). Nucleation of aragonite upon carbonation of calcium oxide and calcium hydroxide at ambient temperatures and pressures: A new indicator of fire-related human activities. *Journal of Archaeological Science*, **49**, 237–48. https://doi.org/10.1016/j.jas.2014.05.020.

Toffolo, M. B., Richard, M. (2024). Infrared spectral library of tooth enamel from African ungulates for accurate electron spin resonance dating. *Scientific Data* **11**(1), 890. https://doi.org/10.1038/s41597-024-03725-y

Toffolo, M. B., Brink, J. S., Berna, F. (2015). Bone diagenesis at the Florisbad spring site, Free State Province (South Africa): Implications for the taphonomy of the Middle and Late Pleistocene faunal assemblages. *Journal of Archaeological Science: Reports*, **4**, 152–63. https://doi.org/10.1016/j.jasrep.2015.09.001.

Toffolo, M. B., Brink, J. S., van Huyssteen, C., *et al.* (2017a). A microstratigraphic reevaluation of the Florisbad spring site, Free State Province, South Africa: Formation processes and paleoenvironment. *Geoarchaeology: An International Journal*, **32(4)**, 456–78. https://doi.org/10.1002/gea.21616.

Toffolo, M. B., Fantalkin, A., Lemos, I. S., *et al.* (2013a). Towards an absolute chronology for the Aegean Iron Age: New radiocarbon dates from Lefkandi, Kalapodi and Corinth. *PLoS ONE*, **8(12)**, e83117. https://doi.org/10.1371/journal.pone.0083117.

Toffolo, M. B., Klein, E., Elbaum, R., *et al.* (2013b). An early Iron Age assemblage of faience beads from Ashkelon, Israel: Chemical composition and manufacturing process. *Journal of Archaeological Science*, **40(10)**, 3626–35. https://doi.org/10.1016/j.jas.2013.05.010.

Toffolo, M., Maeir, A. M., Chadwick, J. R., *et al.* (2012). Characterization of contexts for radiocarbon dating: Results from the Early Iron Age at Tell es-Safi/Gath, Israel. *Radiocarbon*, **54(3–4)**, 371–90. https://doi.org/10.1017/S0033822200047159.

Toffolo, M. B., Martin, M. A. S., Master, D. M., *et al.* (2018). Microarchaeology of a grain silo: Insights into stratigraphy, chronology and food storage at Late Bronze Age Ashkelon, Israel. *Journal of Archaeological Science: Reports*, **19**, 177–88. https://doi.org/10.1016/j.jasrep.2018.02.047.

Toffolo M. B., Pinkas, I., Álvaro Gallo, A., *et al.* (2023a). Crystallinity assessment of anthropogenic calcites using Raman micro-spectroscopy. *Scientific Reports*, **13**, **12971**. https://doi.org/10.1038/s41598-023-39842-8.

Toffolo, M. B., Regev, L., Dubernet, S., *et al.* (2019a). FTIR-based crystallinity assessment of aragonite–calcite mixtures in archaeological lime binders altered by diagenesis. *Minerals*, **9(2)**, **121**. https://doi.org/10.3390/min9020121.

Toffolo, M.B., Regev, L., Mintz, E., *et al.* (2017b). Accurate radiocarbon dating of archaeological ash using pyrogenic aragonite. *Radiocarbon*, **59(1)**, **231–49**. https://doi.org/10.1017/RDC.2017.7.

Toffolo, M. B., Regev, L., Mintz, E., *et al.* (2023b). Micro-contextual characterization of pyrogenic aragonite diagenesis in archaeological ash: Implications for radiocarbon dating of calcium carbonate in combustion features. *Archaeological and Anthropological Sciences*, **15**, **177**. https://doi.org/10.1007/s12520-023-01874-6.

Toffolo, M. B., Regev, L., Mintz, E., *et al.* (2020a). Structural characterization and thermal decomposition of lime binders allow accurate radiocarbon age determinations of aerial lime plaster. *Radiocarbon*, **62(3)**, **633–55**. https://doi.org/10.1017/RDC.2020.39.

Toffolo, M. B., Ricci, G., Caneve, L., *et al.* (2019b). Luminescence reveals variations in local structural order of calcium carbonate polymorphs formed by different mechanisms. *Scientific Reports*, **9**, **16170**. https://doi.org/10.1038/s41598-019-52587-7.

Toffolo, M.B., Ricci, G., Chapoulie, R., *et al.* (2020b). Cathodoluminescence and laser-induced fluorescence of calcium carbonate: A review of screening methods for radiocarbon dating of ancient lime mortars. *Radiocarbon*, **62(3)**, **545–64**. https://doi.org/10.1017/RDC.2020.21.

Toffolo, M. B., Tribolo, C., Horwitz, L. K., *et al.* (2023c). Palaeoenvironments and chronology of the Damvlei Later Stone age site, Free State, South Africa. *South African Archaeological Bulletin*, **78(219)**, **57–74**. https://cnrs.hal.science/hal-04378185/file/TOFFOLO.pdf.

Toffolo, M. B., Ullman, M., Caracuta, V., *et al.* (2017c). A 10,400-year-old sunken lime kiln from the Early Pre-Pottery Neolithic B at the Nesher-Ramla quarry (el-Khirbe), Israel. *Journal of Archaeological Science: Reports*, **14**, **353–64**. https://doi.org/10.1016/j.jasrep.2017.06.014.

Trueman, C. N. G., Behrensmeyer, A. K., Tuross, N., *et al.* (2004). Mineralogical and compositional changes in bones exposed on soil surfaces in Amboseli National Park, Kenya: Diagenetic mechanisms and the role of sediment pore fluids. *Journal of Archaeological Science*, **31**, **721–39**. https://doi.org/10.1016/j.jas.2003.11.003.

Ullman, M., Brailovsky, L., Schechter, H. C., *et al.* (2022). The early Pre-Pottery Neolithic B site at Nesher-Ramla Quarry, Israel. *Quaternary International*, **624**, **148**–67. https://doi.org/10.1016/j.quaint.2021.04.019.

Urbanová, P., Boaretto, E., Artioli, G. (2020). The state-of-the-art of dating techniques applied to ancient mortars and binders: A review. *Radiocarbon*, **62(3)**, **503**–25. https://doi.org/10.1017/RDC.2020.43.

Vagenas, N. V., Gatsouli, A., Kontoyannis, C. G. (2003). Quantitative analysis of synthetic calcium carbonate polymorphs using FT-IR spectroscopy. *Talanta*, **59**, **831**–6. https://doi.org/10.1016/S0039-9140(02)00638-0.

Valla, F., Khalaily, H., Valladas, H., *et al.* (2007). Les fouilles de Ain Mallaha (Eynan) de 2003 à 2005: Quatrième rapport préliminaire. *Journal of the Israel Prehistoric Society*, **37**, 135–379. www.jstor.org/stable/23389906.

van der Marel, H. W., Beutelspacher, H. (1976). *Atlas of Infrared Spectroscopy of Clay Minerals and Their Admixtures*. Amsterdam: Elsevier.

van Hoesel, A., Reidsma, F. H., van Os, B. J. H., *et al.* (2019). Combusted bone: Physical and chemical changes of bone during laboratory simulated heating under oxidising conditions and their relevance for the study of ancient fire use. *Journal of Archaeological Science: Reports*, **28**, **102033**. https://doi.org/10.1016/j.jasrep.2019.102033.

Villagran, X. S., Hartmann, G. A., Stahlschmidt, M., *et al.* (2021). Formation processes of the Late Pleistocene Site Toca da Janela da Barra do Antonião – Piauí (Brazil). *PaleoAmerica*, **7(3)**, **260**–79. https://doi.org/10.1080/20555563.2021.1931744.

Villagran, X. S., Strauss, A., Miller, C., *et al.* (2017). Buried in ashes: Site formation processes at Lapa do Santo rockshelter, east-central Brazil. *Journal of Archaeological Science*, **77**, **10**–34. https://doi.org/10.1016/j.jas.2016.07.008.

Walker, M. J., Anesin, D., Angelucci, D. E., *et al.* (2016). Combustion at the late Early Pleistocene site of Cueva Negra del Estrecho del Río Quípar (Murcia, Spain). *Antiquity*, **90(351)**, **571**–89. https://doi.org/10.15184/aqy.2016.91.

Wang, R. Z., Addadi, L., Weiner, S. (1997). Design strategies of sea urchin teeth: Structure, composition and micromechanical relations to function. *Philosophical Transactions of the Royal Society of London B*, **352**, **469**–80. https://doi.org/10.1098/rstb.1997.0034.

Weiner, S. (2010). *Microarchaeology. Beyond the Visible Archaeological Record*. Cambridge: Cambridge University Press. https://doi.org/10.1017/CBO9780511811210.

Weiner, S., Bar-Yosef, O. (1990). States of preservation of bones from prehistoric sites in the near east: A survey. *Journal of Archaeological Science*, **17**, **187**–96. https://doi.org/10.1016/0305-4403(90)90058-D.

Weiner, S., Berna, F., Cohen, I., *et al.* (2007). Mineral distributions in Kebara Cave: Diagenesis and its effect on the archaeological record. In Bar-Yosef, O., Meignen, L., eds., *Kebara Cave, Mt. Carmel, Israel, Part I.* Cambridge, MA: Harvard University Press, pp. **131**–**46**.

Weiner, S., Brumfeld, V., Marder, O., *et al* (2015). Heating of flint debitage from Upper Palaeolithic contexts at Manot Cave, Israel: Changes in atomic organization due to heating using infrared spectroscopy. *Journal of Archaeological Science*, **54**, **45**–**53**. https://doi.org/10.1016/j.jas.2014.11.023.

Weiner, S., Goldberg, P. (1990). On-site Fourier transform–infrared spectrometry at an archaeological excavation. *Spectroscopy International*, **2(2)**, **39**–**42**.

Weiner, S., Goldberg, P., Bar-Yosef, O. (1993). Bone preservation in Kebara Cave, Israel using on-site Fourier transform infrared spectrometry. *Journal of Archaeological Science*, **20**, **613**–**27**. https://doi.org/10.1006/jasc.1993.1037.

Weiner, S., Goldberg, P., Bar-Yosef, O. (2002). Three-dimensional distribution of minerals in the sediments of Hayonim Cave, Israel: Diagenetic processes and archaeological implications. *Journal of Archaeological Science*, **29(11)**, **1289**–**308**. https://doi.org/10.1006/jasc.2001.0790.

Weiner, S., Nagorsky, A., Taxel, I., *et al.* (2020). High temperature pyrotechnology: A macro- and microarchaeology study of a late Byzantine-beginning of Early Islamic period (7th century CE) pottery kiln from Tel Qatra/Gedera, Israel. *Journal of Archaeological Science: Reports*, **31**, **102263**. https://doi.org/10.1016/j.jasrep.2020.102263.

Weiner, S., Pinkas, I., Kossoy, A., *et al.* (2021). Calcium Sulfate Hemihydrate (Bassanite) crystals in the wood of the *Tamarix* tree. *Minerals*, **11**, 289. https://doi.org/10.3390/min11030289.

Weiner, S., Xu, Q., Goldberg, P., Liu, J., Bar-Yosef, O. (1998). Evidence for the use of fire at Zhoukoudian, China. *Science*, **281**, **251**–**3**. https://doi.org/10.1126/science.281.5374.251.

Wright, L. E., Schwarcz, H. P. (1996). Infrared and isotopic evidence for diagenesis of bone apatite at Dos Pilas, Guatemala: Palaeodietary implications. *Journal of Archaeological Science*, **23**, **933**–**44**. https://doi.org/10.1006/jasc.1996.0087.

Xin, Y., Tepper, Y., Bar-Oz, G., *et al.* (2021). FTIR bone characterization and radiocarbon dating: Timing the abandonment of Byzantine pigeon towers in the Negev Desert, Israel. *Radiocarbon*, **63(6)**, **1715**–**35**. https://doi.org/10.1017/RDC.2021.85.

Xu, B., Hirsch, A., Kronik, L., *et al.* (2018). Vibrational properties of isotopically enriched materials: The case of calcite. *RSC Advances*, **59(8)**, **33985**–**92**. https://doi.org/10.1039/C8RA06608F.

Xu, B., Poduska, K. M. (2014). Linking crystal structure with temperature-sensitive vibrational modes in calcium carbonate minerals. *Physical Chemistry Chemical Physics*, **16**, **17634–39**. https://doi.org/10.1039/C4CP01772B.

Xu, B., Toffolo, M. B., Boaretto, E., *et al.* (2016). Assessing local and long-range structural disorder in aggregate-free lime binders. *Industrial & Engineering Chemistry Research*, **55**, **8334–40**. https://doi.org/10.1021/acs.iecr.6b01785.

Xu, B., Toffolo, M. B., Regev, L., *et al.* (2015). Structural differences in archaeologically relevant calcite. *Analytical Methods*, **7(21)**, **9304–9**. https://doi.org/10.1039/C5AY01942G.

Yizhaq, M., Mintz, G., Cohen, I., *et al.* (2005). Quality controlled radiocarbon dating of bones and charcoal from the early Pre-Pottery Neolithic B (PPNB) of Motza (Israel). *Radiocarbon*, **47(2)**, **193–206**. https://doi.org/10.1017/S003382220001969X.

Yoshioka, S., Kitano, Y. (1985). Transformation of aragonite to calcite through heating. *Geochemical Journal*, **19**, **245–9**. https://doi.org/10.2343/geochemj.19.245.

Zhao, T., Peng, M., Yang, M., *et al.* (2023). Effects of weathering on FTIR spectra and origin traceability of archaeological amber: The case of the Han Tomb of Haihun Marquis, China. *Journal of Archaeological Science*, **153**, **105753**. https://doi.org/10.1016/j.jas.2023.105753.

Acknowledgments

I wish to thank Francesco Berna and Steve Weiner for teaching me infrared spectroscopy. I also would like to thank several colleagues who kindly provided standard materials for the spectral library: Ana Álvaro (beeswax, clay minerals, cristobalite, hematite, limonite, moganite, quartz, serpentine), Ana Isabel Ortega (fossil charcoal), Felipe Cuartero (modern bone, flint, pine tar), Javier Llamazares (limestone), Mario Modesto (fresh charcoal), Teresa Moradillo (wood), Maïlys Richard (paraffin), and Carlos Sáiz (epoxy, polyester). I am grateful to Carla García for recording and editing the videos and to Maïlys Richard for preparing Figure 1. Thanks to Maïlys Richard and Ana Álvaro for reading and commenting on the manuscript. I am also grateful to two anonymous reviewers, who helped improve the manuscript with their comments. Last but not least, I wish to thank Darwin the Italian greyhound, who assisted me throughout most of the writing and reminded me that it is good to take a break.

This work was funded by the European Union (ERC, PEOPLE, project n. 101039711 to Michael Toffolo). Views and opinions expressed are however those of the author only and do not necessarily reflect those of the European Union or the European Research Council. Neither the European Union nor the granting authority can be held responsible for them. Michael Toffolo is supported also by the grant RYC2021-030917-I funded by the MCIN/AEI/10.13039/501100011033 and by the "European Union NextGenerationEU/PRTR."

European Research Council

Established by the European Commission

Cambridge Elements ☰

Current Archaeological Tools and Techniques

Hans Barnard

Cotsen Institute of Archaeology

Hans Barnard was associate adjunct professor in the Department of Near Eastern Languages and Cultures as well as associate researcher at the Cotsen Institute of Archaeology, both at the University of California, Los Angeles. He currently works at the Roman site of Industria in northern Italy and previously participated in archaeological projects in Armenia, Chile, Egypt, Ethiopia, Italy, Iceland, Panama, Peru, Sudan, Syria, Tunisia, and Yemen. This is reflected in the seven books and more than 100 articles and chapters to which he contributed.

Willeke Wendrich

Polytechnic University of Turin

Willeke Wendrich is Professor of Cultural Heritage and Digital Humanities at the Politecnico di Torino (Turin, Italy). Until 2023 she was Professor of Egyptian Archaeology and Digital Humanities at the University of California, Los Angeles, and the first holder of the Joan Silsbee Chair in African Cultural Archaeology. Between 2015 and 2023 she was Director of the Cotsen Institute of Archaeology, with which she remains affiliated. She managed archaeological projects in Egypt, Ethiopia, Italy, and Yemen, and is on the board of the International Association of Egyptologists, Museo Egizio (Turin, Italy), the Institute for Field Research, and the online UCLA Encyclopedia of Egyptology.

About the Series

Cambridge University Press and the Cotsen Institute of Archaeology at UCLA collaborate on this series of Elements, which aims to facilitate deployment of specific techniques by archaeologists in the field and in the laboratory. It provides readers with a basic understanding of selected techniques, followed by clear instructions how to implement them, or how to collect samples to be analyzed by a third party, and how to approach interpretation of the results.

COTSEN INSTITUTE OF
ARCHAEOLOGY AT UCLA

Cambridge Elements ≡

Current Archaeological Tools and Techniques

A full series listing is available at: www.cambridge.org/EATT

Printed in the United States
by Baker & Taylor Publisher Services